W9-AMQ-202

MILESTONES
IN MODERN
WORLD HISTORY

The End of
Apartheid in
South Africa

MILESTONES
IN MODERN WORLD HISTORY

The Bolshevik Revolution

The Chinese Cultural
Revolution

The Collapse of
the Soviet Union

D-Day and the Liberation
of France

The End of Apartheid
in South Africa

The Iranian Revolution

The Treaty of Versailles

The Universal Declaration
of Human Rights

MILESTONES
IN MODERN
WORLD HISTORY

1600 · · · 1750 · ·   · · · 1940 · · · 2000

The End of Apartheid in South Africa

LIZ SONNEBORN

CHELSEA HOUSE
PUBLISHERS
An imprint of Infobase Publishing

The End of Apartheid in South Africa

Chelsea House
An imprint of Infobase Publishing
132 West 31st Street
New York, NY 10001

Library of Congress Cataloging-in-Publication Data

Sonneborn, Liz.
The end of apartheid in South Africa / Liz Sonneborn.
  p. cm.—(Milestones in modern world history)
Includes bibliographical references and index.
ISBN 978-1-60413-409-4 (hardcover)
1. Apartheid—South Africa—History—Juvenile literature. 2. Anti-apartheid movements—South Africa—History—Juvenile literature. 3. South Africa—Race relations—Juvenile literature. I. Title.
DT1757.S66 2009
968.06′4—dc22   2008054805

Chelsea House books are available at special discounts when purchased in bulk quantities for businesses, associations, institutions, or sales promotions. Please call our Special Sales Department in New York at (212) 967-8800 or (800) 322-8755.

You can find Chelsea House on the World Wide Web at http://www.chelseahouse.com.

Text design by Erik Lindstrom
Cover design by Alicia Post
Composition by Keith Trego
Cover printed by Bang Printing, Brainerd, MN
Book printed and bound by Bang Printing, Brainerd, MN
Date printed: December 2010
Printed in the United States of America

10 9 8 7 6 5 4 3

This book is printed on acid-free paper.

All links and Web addresses were checked and verified to be correct at the time of publication. Because of the dynamic nature of the Web, some addresses and links may have changed since publication and may no longer be valid.

CONTENTS

A Walk to Freedom

On February 11, 1990, Nelson Mandela woke up before dawn. He had gone to sleep only a few hours before, but he was too excited to sleep any later. As the sun rose, Mandela looked out his window and saw a cloudless blue sky.

It was going to be a beautiful day. But for Mandela, it would also mark the start of a new phase in his life. He had spent the last 27 years, 6 months, and 7 days in prison. That afternoon, he was finally to be released.

A FAMOUS PRISONER

At the time, Nelson Mandela was the most famous political prisoner in the world. In the early 1960s, he had risen to prominence in the African National Congress (ANC), a political organization in the country of South Africa. The

Nelson and Winnie Mandela walk triumphantly through the streets of Cape Town, following his release from prison on February 11, 1990. Nelson Mandela had been imprisoned for more than a quarter-century.

ANC vehemently opposed the South African government policies known as apartheid. Through apartheid, the government tried to keep all political and economic power in the hands of the nation's white minority, the Afrikaners. As a result, black South Africans, who made up the majority of the population, were treated terribly. Every day, they faced legal discrimination under an unjust government that controlled every aspect of their lives—from where they could live to what jobs they could hold to whom they could marry.

Fiery and forthright, Mandela spoke out against the apartheid government and its horrendous treatment of black South Africans. The government struck back by charging him with sabotage. In 1964, Mandela was convicted and sentenced to life in prison. Though Mandela was silenced, he was not forgotten. Activists who fought against South Africa's racist rule continued to invoke his name as an honored martyr for their cause. Over time, the anti-apartheid movement grew, both within South Africa and abroad. By the start of the 1990s, internal and external opposition had nearly brought the South African government to its knees.

DE KLERK'S ANNOUNCEMENT

To avoid a complete collapse, President F.W. de Klerk decided to push for substantial political reforms. On February 2, 1990, he announced his plans to the parliament, South Africa's law-making body. De Klerk called for an end to the government's ban on the ANC and other political groups. He also declared that many long-held political prisoners, including the now internationally revered Mandela, would be freed.

It was not the first time the government had offered to release Mandela. Starting in 1985, freedom was periodically dangled before Mandela, but always with the condition that he reject the actions of the ANC. He steadfastly refused the offers. This time, however, de Klerk promised to release Mandela without requiring anything in return.

South Africans who were opposed to apartheid—black and white alike—were thrilled by the news. Throughout the country, they rejoiced that Mandela soon would be set free. For decades, he had been an almost mythic figure, a symbol of the entire anti-apartheid resistance movement. Now his supporters would finally be able to get to know Mandela the man.

Across the country, people speculated about Mandela. What did he look like? Had his many years in prison changed him? When they got the chance to see him again and hear him speak, would Mandela live up to his reputation as a great leader, or would he be a disappointment?

(continues on page 12)

NELSON MANDELA

Nelson Mandela was born on July 18, 1918, in the village of Mvezo. His parents gave him the first name Rolihlahla, meaning "pulling the branch of a tree." While attending a mission school, he became known by the English name Nelson.

After graduating from high school, Nelson Mandela continued his education at the University College of Fort Hare. He was suspended from college for participating in a student boycott to protest the South African government's policies. With his cousin, Mandela ran away to the city of Johannesburg to escape an arranged marriage planned by his family. There, he studied law and joined the African National Congress (ANC) in 1943. Mandela also married Evelyn Mase. The couple had four children before divorcing in 1958. Shortly afterward, he married his second wife, Winnie, with whom he had two daughters.

In 1944, Mandela joined with several other young ANC members to form the Congress Youth League (CYL). They wanted to shake up the conservative ANC, which they believed needed to be more aggressive in fighting for the civil rights of black South Africans. Mandela was instrumental in drafting the Program of Action in 1949. The plan, as adopted by the ANC, called for boycotts, strikes, and non-violent defiance against the new policy of apartheid.

In the early 1950s, the government began harassing Mandela. He was put on trial several times, banned from attending any political gatherings, and prohibited from leaving Johannesburg. During this period, Mandela started the first black law firm in South Africa with fellow ANC leader Oliver Tambo. In 1955, Mandela was one of 156 political activists arrested in a government crackdown against alleged Communists. Thirty were put on trial, although the case was thrown out of court more than five years later. In the 1960s, the government banned the ANC, and Mandela was forced to live underground and adopt a series of disguises to evade arrest. During this time, he became the commander in chief of the Umkhonto we Sizwe, the new militant wing of the ANC. Its mission was to bomb government buildings and commit other acts of sabotage to force the government to abandon apartheid policies. Mandela also left South Africa for a few months. He toured England and other countries, giving speeches to promote the anti-apartheid cause. Soon after he returned, he was arrested for illegally leaving the country and for inciting an unlawful strike. Mandela was convicted and sentenced to five years in prison.

Because of his connection with the Umkhonto we Sizwe, Mandela was charged with sabotage in 1963. He and other arrested ANC leaders defended themselves at the eight-month Rivonia trial. Mandela delivered an impassioned speech in which he stated that he was willing to die for his political beliefs. He was found guilty and sentenced to life in prison. For 27 years, Mandela remained behind bars. Several times, the government offered him an early release, but only if he spoke out in favor of its policies or renounced the ANC's use of violent protest. Every time, Mandela refused.

In early 1990, President F.W. de Klerk promised to reform South Africa's apartheid policies and showed his commitment to change by releasing Mandela from jail. As president of the ANC, Mandela immediately began to help shape the new post-apartheid South Africa. For his efforts, he, along with de Klerk, received the Nobel Peace Prize in 1993. In April 1994, South Africa held its first election in which all citizens, regardless of their race, were permitted to vote.

(continues)

(continued)

The ANC's slate of candidates won the most votes. The new ANC-dominated parliament then elected Nelson Mandela as the first black president of South Africa. During his administration, Mandela struggled to rebuild the country's ailing economy, which had been severely damaged by apartheid.

After one presidential term, Mandela retired from politics in 1999. Revered the world over for his courage and compassion, he has since remained active in many causes. He also established the Nelson Mandela Foundation, an organization dedicated to promoting human rights and social justice.

(continued from page 9)
WAITING FOR NEWS

The excitement that radiated through South Africa after de Klerk's announcement soon began to flag. Days passed, and Mandela still remained imprisoned. His supporters feared that de Klerk's words were no more than that. Perhaps the president had not really meant what he said. Perhaps he would not keep his promise after all.

At the same time, pro-apartheid Afrikaners were steaming over de Klerk's declaration. Some of their leaders openly talked about overthrowing de Klerk's regime. Members of one pro-apartheid group, the Afrikaner Resistance Movement, protested against his proposed reforms. Marching through the streets of Pretoria, South Africa's administrative capital, they chanted "Hang Mandela!" to intimidate his supporters.

To quell the agitation of both sides, de Klerk summoned Mandela to his office on February 10. He said Mandela would be freed the next day. Mandela argued with the president. The ANC had appointed a reception committee to organize a mass celebration of his release. The committee needed another week to make plans. De Klerk refused to give the ANC any more time. Mandela, in turn, refused any protection from the government's police force. Even though pro-apartheid groups had threatened his life, he did not want his supporters to believe he was beholden to de Klerk's regime in any way.

That night, reception committee members met with Mandela. Together, they drafted a speech he would deliver the next day in the nearby city of Cape Town. His friend and attorney Dullah Omar later described Mandela's mood. Contemplating the end of his decades of imprisonment, Mandela sat "subdued, quiet, deep in thought."[1]

PLANNING MANDELA'S RELEASE

The next morning, Mandela still remained calm. After sunrise, he had his breakfast and met with the prison doctor for a prerelease exam. He then packed up his belongings—mostly books and papers—in about a dozen crates. In his final hours of confinement, Mandela told Omar that he was overwhelmed with excitement, but "he showed no emotion. He was very composed."[2]

The ANC had carefully mapped out Mandela's first afternoon as a free man. ANC associates, including his wife Winnie, were flying in from the city of Johannesburg in two chartered planes and would arrive at the prison at 3:00 that afternoon. Outside its gates, Mandela would get in a chauffeured car bound for Cape Town. There, he would deliver his speech on a balcony overlooking a great outdoor plaza known as the Grand Parade.

As Mandela waited inside, a huge crowd gathered around the prison gate. Some onlookers climbed up trees, hoping to get the best view of Mandela as he stepped outside. Newspaper reporters and television news crews scrambled to ready themselves for his appearance. They would broadcast the release live, not only throughout South Africa, but around the world.

The ANC's planes were late. Outside the prison, everyone became antsy as 3:00 came and went with no sight of Mandela. Inside, Mandela, too, grew impatient. In his autobiography, he recalled telling the reception committee that "my people had been waiting for me for twenty-seven years and I did not want to keep them waiting any longer."[3]

AT THE PRISON GATE

Finally, Mandela's ANC colleagues and Winnie arrived. At about 3:45, the people gathered at the prison caught their first glimpse of Mandela as he headed toward the gate. They saw a tall and slender 71-year-old man wearing a gray suit, carrying himself with great dignity as he walked hand in hand with his loyal wife. At the same time, Mandela took in the scene before him. He had expected a few dozen spectators, but now he faced a crowd of thousands. "I was astounded and a little bit alarmed,"[4] he later remembered.

About 20 feet (6 meters) from the gate, he was overwhelmed with "a noise that sounded like some great herd of metallic beasts."[5] It was the sound of photographers clicking their cameras, while reporters shouted their questions to Mandela. A television crew shoved "a long, dark, furry object"[6] at him. He jolted, instinctively thinking the strange thing was some kind of weapon. Knowing how unfamiliar he was with modern technology after his long incarceration, Winnie quickly explained it was a microphone.

In the chaos of the moment, Mandela also heard the clamoring of the crowd. He raised his right fist high in the air as a victory salute to celebrate his freedom and his cause. "I had not been able to do that for twenty-seven years," Mandela later wrote, "and it gave me a surge of strength and joy."[7] His supporters responded with an ear-shattering cheer.

THE CROWD IN CAPE TOWN

Within minutes, the jubilant Mandela was shepherded into a sedan, which sped off to Cape Town. The driver took back roads to avoid any security problems. From the window, Mandela spied lush farms and vineyards and marveled at the lovely landscapes of his homeland. He also saw his supporters lined up along the roadside, waving as his car whizzed by. To Mandela's surprise, most were white farmers. He had not realized that so many white South Africans had joined the anti-apartheid movement. "It made me think that the South Africa I was returning to was far different from the one I had left,"[8] Mandela explained.

At the Grand Parade, there were still more surprises awaiting Mandela. When his car reached the outskirts of Cape Town, he watched throngs of supporters pouring into the city. For hours, people had been flocking to the Grand Parade to see Mandela make his first speech as a free man.

Mandela's car was supposed to circle around to the back of the old city hall building, where he was scheduled to speak. But the driver instead drove toward the front entrance. In an instant, the car was mobbed. People gathered around it on all sides; some jumped on the hood. Mandela remained calm, although, as the car jolted from side to side, he feared "the crowd might very well kill us with their love."[9] He sat "imprisoned by thousands of our own supporters"[10] for almost an hour before a path could be cleared.

MANDELA SPEAKS

At dusk, Mandela finally emerged from the city hall balcony, ready to speak to the enthusiastic crowd of an estimated 250,000 people. As he remembered, he walked out and "saw a boundless sea of people cheering, holding flags and banners, clapping, and laughing."[11] Once again, he raised his fist in the air, prompting his audience to shout out loud and long in celebration. Mandela then pulled his speech from his breast pocket and in a mild yet firm tone let his words wash over the crowd.

Mandela began by reminding his listeners that he was not a "prophet."[12] He was merely a "humble servant of you, the people."[13] He thanked all his supporters in South Africa and

Nelson Mandela's former prison cell on Robben Island, South Africa, where he spent most of his incarceration.

throughout the rest of the world for tirelessly lobbying for his release.

Mandela then turned his attention to apartheid. "Today the majority of South Africans, black and white, recognize that apartheid has no future,"[14] he told the crowd. He reminded them how apartheid had shattered families, left millions impoverished and homeless, and fueled political strife that endangered the entire nation.

Mandela also said that recognizing these truths was not enough. It was now time for the anti-apartheid movement to "intensify the struggle on all fronts"[15] and for all involved to "redouble our efforts."[16] To the de Klerk government's dismay, Mandela did not condemn violence as a means to combat apartheid, but he acknowledged it as a necessary part of the ongoing fight. Mandela concluded with words he first spoke in 1964, during the trial that ended with his prison sentence: "I have cherished the ideal of a democratic and free society in which all persons live together in harmony and with equal opportunities. . . . If needs be, it is an ideal for which I am prepared to die."[17]

Nelson Mandela's release from prison was a momentous event in twentieth-century history. It is still commemorated in South Africa and beyond as a historic moment. Mandela's release finally ended an enormous injustice. Perhaps more importantly, it also symbolized the beginning of the end of apartheid. When apartheid's vicious and cruel policies finally were dismantled in South Africa, not only Mandela, but also an entire nation was at last set free.

Under Dutch
and British Rule

In 1652, ships belonging to the Dutch East India Company—
a trading operation that shipped goods between Europe and
Asia—sailed through treacherous waters to reach the Cape of
Good Hope at the southern tip of Africa. Once ashore, the
company's employees constructed a small fort, which served
as a base where the company's ships could stop off and replen-
ish their supplies during the long journey.

Historians often refer to the establishment of the Dutch
fort as the beginning of South Africa. Yet long before these
immigrants from the Dutch Republic (now the Netherlands)
arrived, the region had been settled by various groups of native
African tribes. In fact, cave paintings and other prehistoric
records suggest that human beings had been living in present-
day South Africa for more than 20,000 years.

The Landing of Jan van Riebeeck, an 1850 painting by Charles Bell, depicts the Dutch arrival at the Cape of Good Hope in South Africa in 1652.

The earliest peoples there survived by hunting, fishing, and gathering wild foods. By the mid-seventeenth century, the region was primarily inhabited by the San people, who remained hunter-gatherers. Other groups who had moved into present-day South Africa included the Khoikhoi, who were chiefly cattle herders, and the Bantu speakers, who increasingly relied on farming to obtain food. These various native groups helped to make the region the most socially and economically diverse in all of Africa.

NATIVES AND NEWCOMERS

From the start, the Dutch newcomers showed little respect for the natives they encountered. For example, they traded for cattle with the Khoikhoi but quickly annoyed the herders by planting fields of grain on their traditional grazing grounds. (Slaves imported from Asia and other areas of Africa operated the Dutch farms.)

As the settlement grew, conflicts broke out between the Dutch and the Khoikhoi. Each side staged raids to steal cattle and other goods from the other. In this ongoing battle, the Dutch had one crucial advantage. They had guns—weapons that were unknown to the Khoikhoi before the arrival of the newcomers. The Dutch used their superior weaponry to sub-due the Khoikhoi living near their settlement. By the 1670s, many Khoikhoi were reduced to working alongside imported slaves on Dutch farms.

The clashes between the natives and the Dutch continued as the Dutch started moving inland from the coast. Throughout the 1700s, the San and the Khoikhoi violently resisted the Dutch incursions into their lands. The Dutch responded with their own violence and often took African women and children captive to work as laborers and servants. The Dutch also tried to restrict the movements of native peoples: Africans were not allowed in certain areas unless they had official passes issued by the Dutch.

REBELLING AGAINST THE DUTCH

In the eighteenth century, the Dutch presence in the Cape Colony grew primarily because they had large families. Dutch immigration to the colony, however, was slow. Non-Dutch immigrants from Europe, mainly German and French Protes-tants who had left their homeland to escape religious persecu-tion, did help to augment the white population in South Africa. Often, European men of the Cape Colony impregnated African slaves or Khoikhoi women. The children of these unions cre-ated a new, distinct class in the settlement.

For almost 150 years, the Dutch East India Company ruled the Cape Colony. During that time, it doled out rights and privileges according to a strict hierarchy based on race. At the top of the social ladder were the company's employees. Directly below them were the other European settlers. Next came the mixed-race population, and at the bottom were the slaves.

Even as the Dutch were establishing their hierarchy, the native population continued to resist Dutch control. In 1799, the Khoikhoi and San laborers in the Cape Colony deserted their farms and began battling the Dutch, hoping to reclaim their territory from these intruders. They allied themselves with the chiefs of the Xhosa people, who also had fought the Dutch when they tried to encroach on the Xhosa's lands.

THE BRITISH ARRIVE

After years of war, a third group entered the fray. Immigrants from Great Britain arrived in southern Africa, determined to take over the trade route to Asia. The British succeeded not only in putting down the rebellion of the allied natives, but they also managed to wrestle control of the Cape Colony from the Dutch.

The British knew the Dutch resented the takeover. To keep their colony running smoothly, they tried to accommodate the needs of the Dutch settlers. The British were far less generous in their dealings with the native rebels. They unleashed an army to end the Xhosa resistance once and for all by slaughtering as many native warriors as possible. The British governor of the colony wrote to his superiors in Great Britain that only a hideous bloodbath would "impress on the minds of these savages a proper degree of terror and respect."[1]

For many years, humanitarians in Great Britain had decried the use of slaves in British colonies around the world. In 1807, following many years of intense lobbying by abolitionists, the British Parliament passed the Slave Trade Act, which made the slave trade illegal in any land that Great Britain controlled. In 1833, the Slavery Abolition Act banned slavery throughout the majority of the British Empire. As a result, slaves were techni-

The Great Trek, a twentieth-century painting by James Edwin McConnell, portrays the Boers' departure from the Cape Colony so they could continue to enslave the native population and be free of British control.

cally freed in the Cape Colony in 1833, but they remained subject to such severe restrictions that their relationship with their former masters barely changed.

THE BOER REPUBLICS

Even though blacks remained virtual slaves after their liberation, the Dutch settlers were angry. They disapproved of the abolition of slavery and feared it would put the poorest white Christians on the same social and economic level as the freed black slaves. The settlers, known as the Boers (the Dutch word for "farmers"), also were upset about British land policies. The Boers were not allowed to own land, and many were deeply indebted to their British landlords.

In protest, about 15,000 Boers left the Cape Colony and moved to lands to the north and west in 1838. Their migration became known as the Great Trek. The Trekkers wanted to establish their own settlements, where they could practice slavery and remain free of British control. They created three independent states—Transorangia (later called the Orange Free State or Free State), Transvaal (later called the South African Republic), and the Natalia Republic.

The Natalia Republic blocked British access to the sea. To regain this territory, British troops invaded Natalia and took control. In 1843, it became the British colony of Natal. There, the British established sugar plantations, worked by laborers imported from India. The other two states, however, remained under Boer rule. In both, the conservative governments sought to enforce the old hierarchy that kept whites at the top and blacks on the bottom of the social order. The 1858 constitution of Transvaal recognized the Boers' "desire to permit no equality between colored people and the white inhabitants of the country, either in church or state."[2]

The Boer governments, however, were fairly weak. African chiefs still held great sway over land use and trade in these regions. Nevertheless, the Boers in the independent states began to think of themselves as a separate and free people. They developed their own society and culture, which was largely based on their shared distaste for their two great enemies—the British, who tried to exert control over them, and the native Africans, who continued to resist the Boers' encroachment on their territory.

A DISCOVERY OF DIAMONDS

By the mid-1860s, present-day South Africa was occupied by the British, the Boers, and black Africans of various tribal groups. There was also a population of mixed-race people and of immigrant workers from India. All these people lived in several, sometimes overlapping, political units. There were two British colonies—the Cape and Natal. There were two Boer republics—the Orange Free State and the South African Republic (Transvaal). And there were several large African chiefdoms. Despite their uneasiness with one another, these peoples and states managed to coexist in the same region.

This delicate balance was upended in 1867 when diamonds were discovered in what is now the city of Kimberley in the province of Northern Cape. Previously, the British in South

THE DEFEAT OF THE ZULU

By the late 1870s, the greatest threat to British control over South Africa was the rise of the Zulu nation. Under the leadership of Cetshwayo, the Zulu tribe had become a great military power. The Zulu considered themselves a sovereign people. They refused to surrender their autonomy to the British.

In January 1879, the British decided to take control of Zululand by force. The invasion was a disaster. The Zulu scored a great victory over the British troops at the Battle of Isandlwana. After the Zulu staged a second attack at Rorke's Drift the following day, the British army was forced to retreat. Stunned by their defeat, the British realized that they had grossly underestimated the Zulu. For the Zulu, however, the victory came at a high price. They lost a large number of warriors, which left them more vulnerable to their enemies.

Determined to restore their pride and to defeat the Zulu once and for all, the British in South Africa sent for reinforcements. The new army, the largest contingent of British troops ever assembled in South Africa, returned to Zululand in April and reached the Zulu capital in July. The two forces came together at the Battle of Ulundi. This time, the British were ready for the great Zulu army. They succeeded in killing more than 1,000 Zulu warriors and capturing Cetshwayo.

Much of the British victory was due to their superior weaponry. They came to Ulundi well equipped with rifles

Africa had struggled to keep their settlements afloat. Now for the first time, they had a valuable natural resource, one that would attract many new immigrants and large amounts of foreign investment. The diamond discovery also changed the British settlers' attitudes toward native South Africans. Many

The 1879 Battle of Isandlwana during the Anglo-Zulu War was a devastating defeat for the British army at the hands of the Zulu people.

and Gatling guns—an early type of machine gun. Although the Zulu had some guns, they relied on their traditional spears to fight the enemy. As they rushed toward the British, hoping to get within stabbing range, many Zulu were mowed down by the relentless gunfire. The warriors also discovered, often too late, that their cowhide shields provided almost no protection from British bullets.

The Zulu continued to hold some sway in South Africa after the Battle of Ulundi, but their military power was greatly reduced. Famine, epidemic disease, and internal divisions further weakened them. By the end of the century, Zululand was completely under British control.

British wanted to cultivate the trust of blacks because they saw them as either potential business partners or purchasers of British-made products. After the discovery of diamonds, however, the British viewed natives as little more than cheap laborers who could be forced to work in the diamond mines. The British immediately concocted harsh policies aimed at exploiting black South Africans by compelling them to perform hard labor at low wages.

As part of this plan, Britain aggressively warred with the remaining South African tribal groups that had retained some degree of economic independence. The most fearsome were the Zulu, a powerful people living near Natal. When the British invaded Zululand in 1879, the Zulu were easily outmatched as they battled British guns with their handmade spears. Even so, the Zulu managed a spectacular victory over British troops at the Battle of Isandlwana. The people of Natal were horrified. They could not believe the Zulu had succeeded in crushing the British army. The British, however, continued the war by bringing in a massive wave of reinforcements. In the end, the British managed to defeat the Zulu and incorporate most of their lands into Natal.

GOLD IN TRANSVAAL

In 1886, the world's largest deposit of gold was discovered in Transvaal. Even more than the diamond discovery, finding gold in South Africa changed the dynamic among the various peoples there. For black Africans, the discovery led to even greater subjugation and humiliation. Barred from owning land or working in skilled professions, they were again forced into the mines. Often their wages were not enough to keep their families fed and clothed. Stranded in poor rural areas, the miners' wives and children had to struggle to survive on the meager wages the men managed to send back to them.

For the Boers, the discovery of gold was a serious threat to their independence. The Boer government of Transvaal reaped some benefit by levying taxes on the gold mines, which were owned by British businessmen. Most of the gold was found in thin veins buried deep within rock faces. Excavating it was a technological challenge requiring large and costly machinery. The Boers were generally too poor to start or operate such expensive mining enterprises. As a result, most of the profits from the mines were sent back to Great Britain rather than being invested in South Africa. The Boers resented that they saw so little of the money that "their" gold was generating.

The British mine owners likewise resented the Boers. Unsurprisingly, they did not like paying taxes to the Transvaal government. They also were annoyed that the government had not constructed enough roads and bridges in mining areas and had refused to pass all the labor laws the British wanted. The wealthy and powerful mine owners were desperate to have more influence over Transvaal and how it was governed. They became convinced the only way that would happen was if the British grabbed control over the region from the Boers.

In 1895, several mine owners concocted a plot to overthrow the Transvaal government. A small army, led by L.S. Jameson, invaded the Boer nation, but it was quickly captured by the Boers. The Jameson Raid was not only an embarrassment for its instigators. It also brought the tension bubbling between the British and the Boers to a boiling point.

THE SOUTH AFRICAN WAR

To protect Transvaal's independence, its president, Paul Kruger, decided on a bold course of action. He declared war on the British. Kruger hoped the Boers could defeat them fast, before they could send for more troops from Great Britain. With the support of the Orange Free State, a Boer force invaded British-held Natal and the Cape Colony in October 1899. The Boers strongly supported Kruger's war. Many were poor farmers whose livelihoods already were threatened by recent droughts and epidemics. They depended on assistance

In this 1900 photograph, Boer families are seen in a British concentration camp at Eshowe Zululand during the Boer War. Through this first use of civilian internment during wartime, the British sought to deprive Boer insurgents of the food and supplies they were obtaining from civilians.

from their government for their survival. If the British took control, they were likely to lose even this modest support.

Both sides hoped for a quick and decisive win. Instead, the war dragged on for three long years. Initially, the Boer militiamen outnumbered the British soldiers two to one. As a result, the Boers seemed poised for victory. The British, however, decided to commit an enormous investment of money and men to secure control over southern Africa. In the end, they sent about 500,000 soldiers to battle the Boers.

Now outnumbered, the Boers began a brutal guerrilla campaign, which the large and well-trained British army seemed powerless to put down. Even after British reinforcements had captured the major cities, the guerrilla resistance continued to surge. The British then decided to wear down the Boer fighters by attacking the civilian population. They burned down Boer farms and fields and slaughtered their herds of livestock. During the ruthless scourge, the British destroyed more than 30,000 farmsteads. In both urban and rural areas, the British also gathered up about 110,000 Boer civilians and about 115,000 black Africans and sent them to concentration camps. Approximately 26,000 Boers and 14,000 black Africans died in these camps. The majority were women and children.

In May 1902, the South African War (also known as the Boer War) came to an end. The Boers were forced to surrender, but the peace agreement, the Treaty of Vereeniging, was fairly kind to them. The British agreed to compensate Boer farmers for their losses. The treaty also stipulated that while the two Boer republics would become colonies of the British Empire, their citizens would be allowed to govern themselves at the local level.

BLACK AFRICANS AND THE POSTWAR ERA

After the war, black Africans hoped that they would receive better treatment from the government. Thousands had been forced to fight or aid troops on both sides of the conflict. They believed both the Boers and the British owed them a debt of gratitude for joining the war effort. The British victory also gave Africans a cause for hope. In the run-up to the war, the British justified their campaign against the Boers by citing the Boers' mistreatment of blacks. The British said they would finally put an end to discriminatory policies against Africans in the Boer republics.

In the war's immediate aftermath, some Africans were able to reclaim their old farms. Because of a postwar labor shortage, many black laborers also saw their wages rise. But these gains were short lived. Once the Boers organized their local governments, they declared that only whites would be able to vote in the Boer-dominated colonies. This move ensured that power would continue to rest in the hands of the white minority.

At the same time, the British took action to stop black South Africans from seeing any rise in their social or economic status. They created policies that forced African farmers off their land and into wage work. The British also dealt with the labor shortage by importing tens of thousands of Chinese workers. As a result, the British could ignore native laborers' demands for higher wages.

It soon became clear that, despite what the British had said before the war, they had no more interest in the rights of black South Africans than the Boers did. In fact, one of the few things the British and Boers could agree on was their mutual desire to oppress black workers. Both groups benefited greatly from the cheap labor of blacks. They also both shared the fear that if native blacks were not completely subdued, the black majority would rebel against the white minority in South Africa.

Out of these twin desires, the Union of South Africa was born in 1910. This country, which had roughly the borders of modern South Africa, was composed of four regions—Transvaal, the Orange Free State, Natal, and the Cape Colony. Its constitution embraced the concept of white supremacy—the idea that white people are inherently superior to people of other races. No blacks were given the right to vote except for a small number of property owners in the Cape Colony. Although the British and the Boers still despised each other, they were willing to share power, however uneasily, to make sure that whites would retain their control over blacks.

3

The Seeds of Apartheid

Almost immediately after its formation, the government of the Union of South Africa began passing laws designed to benefit the country's white population. Less than 20 percent of South Africans were white. These new laws, however, would guarantee that they would hold the reins of power in South Africa.

One of the first of these discriminatory laws was the Natives Land Act of 1913, which gave whites control over almost all farmland in South Africa. The act prohibited black South Africans from purchasing or leasing land outside certain designated areas, which were called reserves. The reserves made up only 7 percent of the nation's land base. In addition, the small amount of land available to blacks was generally of very poor quality. As a result, blacks could no longer operate

small farms—one of the only means they had had for rais-
ing their standard of living. The law, therefore, helped white
farmers by eliminating competition from blacks. Black farmers
were forced to work for whites for far less money than they had
previously made. The act also benefited the owners of mines
and factories. Unable to make a living off their own land, many
blacks who had resisted wage work now had no other way to
earn a livelihood.

JOBS AND HOUSING

The South African government also began regulating mining
and industrial jobs. In the early days of the country's mining
industry, skilled jobs were filled by experienced mine workers
from other countries. These imported workers commanded
high salaries. By the early twentieth century, when a few black
laborers had acquired enough on-the-job training to take on
skilled work, the mine owners happily replaced the higher-paid
foreign experts with lower-paid native talent. This new policy
outraged white mine workers, who resented blacks taking these
coveted jobs. To pacify them, the South African parliament
passed the Mines and Works Act in 1911. It stated that only
whites could hold skilled jobs.

Also in 1911, the parliament passed the Native Labour
Regulation Act. It established rules for recruiting rural blacks
to work in urban areas. Black workers were fingerprinted and
issued special passes, which they had to present before the
authorities would allow them to enter cities. Rural blacks also
were asked to sign employment contracts for urban jobs. If
black workers tried to quit their jobs, thereby breaking the
contract, they could be arrested and sentenced to two months
of hard labor.

The living conditions of black urban workers were harsh.
By the 1920s, many lived in compounds built by companies to
house their black employees. These facilities were crowded and
unsanitary. Black workers also often had to buy food and goods

from company-run stores at inflated prices. As more blacks arrived in towns and cities, some moved into rented housing. White city dwellers were alarmed by the arrival of so many poor blacks. Property owners were especially concerned about the growth of slums, which they feared would drive down the value of their buildings.

The panic led the government to pass the Natives (Urban Areas) Act of 1923. The law formalized housing segregation in South Africa's cities. Black workers had to stay in black-only neighborhoods called townships. If they overstayed the period stipulated in their employment agreements, they could be sent to prison or forced to return to rural reserves, which were plagued by poverty, disease, and malnutrition. According to the law, blacks were permitted to remain in cities only to "minister to the needs of the white population."[1]

RESISTING WHITE RULE

Throughout the early twentieth century, the black population fought against the regulations the South African government placed on just about every aspect of their lives. They formed a variety of organizations to protest against discriminatory laws and to demand basic civil rights. One of the largest was the South African Native National Congress (SANNC), which was founded in 1912 during a meeting of several hundred educated, middle-class blacks in the city of Bloemfontein. (The organization was later renamed the African National Congress, or ANC.)

The SANNC's first president, John L. Dube, was a minister and schoolteacher. While studying in the United States, he became familiar with the work of Booker T. Washington, an African-American educator who counseled American blacks to work hard to achieve economic success, rather than to fight for their rights through the political process. Like Washington, the members of the SANNC were not revolutionaries looking to tear down the political and social system that oppressed

Marcus Garvey, the Jamaican-born activist who called on black Americans to migrate to Africa and start a new nation there, inspired the Wellington Movement of the 1920s in South Africa.

them. Instead, they were reformers seeking to change the South African government by appealing to their countrymen's morality—or as Dube said, "the sense of common justice and love of freedom so innate in the British character."[2] In its early years, the SANNC's approach did not have much effect. For instance, in 1914, the SANNC sent a delegation to London to speak out against the Natives Land Act. British officials dismissed the group by saying there was nothing the government could do about it.

The Wellington Movement of the late 1920s took a more radical approach. Adherents of this movement, named after its leader, Wellington Butelezi, not only wanted black South Africans to remain segregated from white society, they also called on blacks to fight for liberation from their white oppressors. Like the SANNC, the Wellington Movement drew inspiration from a foreign black leader, in this case Marcus Garvey. Born in Jamaica, the charismatic Garvey had started a movement within the United States that called for African Americans to migrate to Africa and establish their own nation there. The Wellington Movement unsuccessfully sought the help of African Americans. The movement's leaders had hoped these new emigrants would lead South Africa's black majority in its fight for liberation.

Opposition to white rule also emerged in rural black churches. Many rural blacks criticized their local chiefs, whom they saw as puppets of the South African government. For leadership they instead looked to their clergy members, many of whom had rejected traditional churches and founded their own in the early twentieth century. These clergy members questioned the authority of officials in the South African government. The government often resorted to violence to suppress their views. For instance, in 1921, Prime Minister Jan Smuts ordered soldiers to remove a religious group called the Israelites from their village. At least 183 blacks were killed in the confrontation.

LABOR TROUBLES

Black labor leaders also repeatedly resisted laws that discriminated against black workers. They frequently called for labor strikes, during which black workers refused to work until their

Jan Christian Smuts served as prime minister of South Africa from 1919 until 1924 and from 1939 until 1948. Although he supported racial segregation, his government issued the 1948 Fagan Report, which stated that complete segregation was not practical. That same year, his party narrowly lost the general election to the National Party, which created the formal system of apartheid.

employers met their demands. In 1920, representatives from various black labor organizations came together to form a labor union of skilled and unskilled workers. Called the Industrial and Commercial Workers' Union (ICU), it had more than 100,000 members at its height.

The same year, black mine workers staged a major strike. To end the protest, mine owners agreed to allow some blacks to hold skilled jobs. This change in policy enraged white workers, who responded with their own strike in 1922. During that latter strike, known as the Rand Revolt, the South African government sided with the employers. Prime Minister Smuts sent in armed soldiers to end the dispute. They killed hundreds of strikers before the workers relented.

The violence, however, made many white workers turn against the Smuts government. In the election of 1924, they voted Smuts out and put in power what came to be known as the Pact Government, because it was made up of representatives from the Labour Party and the National Party. Founded in 1914, the National Party was supported mostly by rural working-class Afrikaners, a term used to describe non-British South African whites of mostly Dutch heritage.

During the 1930s, the South African economy went into a tailspin as the Great Depression caused the prices of diamonds and gold to plunge worldwide. A prolonged drought also threatened South Africa's ranching and farming industries, which caused the living conditions in the rural reserves to deteriorate even further. The crisis was so great that the government passed a new land act that increased the size of the reserves from 7 to 13.5 percent of the nation's land base. But the action did little to relieve the appalling poverty of most reserve residents. In order to survive, many people had no choice but to move to a city in search of wage work. As a result, South Africa's urban population tripled between 1904 and 1936.

The rural poverty of the 1930s also devastated the Afrikaner population. Like poor blacks, many impoverished Afrikaners

started flocking to cities. There, they were upset to find themselves in competition with blacks for low-paying jobs. Many
Afrikaners were outraged. Because they saw blacks as their
inferiors, they believed they should be given preference for jobs

AN AFRICAN AMERICAN
IN SOUTH AFRICA

Recipient of the 1950 Nobel Peace Prize, Ralph Bunche was
one of the most important American diplomats of the twentieth century. Early in his career, Bunche was a member of
the faculties of Harvard University and Howard University,
where he taught political science. While still a professor,
Bunche journeyed to South Africa in 1937. For three months,
he toured the country, all the while keeping detailed notes
about how the experiences of black South Africans compared
with his own as an African American. The following excerpt
from his journal describes several political speeches he
heard in the Grand Parade, the huge, open plaza in the city
of Cape Town:

> Heard a fattish, bald, dark-brown Negro soap-boxing at
> the Parade. He apparently represents the African National
> Congress. . . . Used American Negro as an example con-
> stantly. Said they have brains and wealth and don't stand
> for foolishness. Says American Negro says Africa belongs
> to Africans, and are ready to come back home, but are
> Africans ready to receive them? . . . Says Indians are chas-
> ing the white man out of India and African must regain
> his own country too. Says if white man "doesn't play the
> game" he will be chased out. . . . Said American Negroes
> can strike, but South African natives can't and warned that
> being dressed up didn't make a person a human being.

over black workers. Afrikaners were equally angry at the power wielded by British South Africans. Most of the nation's mines and banks were still owned by the British, giving them a tight rein over South Africa's economy.

American Negro demanded to be treated as human beings and are equal of any people in the world. Praised [African-American boxer] Joe Louis as a great man—a black man and world champion. No white man in all of Africa can challenge him.

Attacked [South African prime minister] Smuts. Said natives must join organizations and use their power. Crowd snickered as he began, but he soon had many nodding their heads in approbation. He spoke vigorously and often cursed. A few white[s] stood by listening; others walked boldly back and forth between him and the crowd. . . . Police not far away, but they didn't molest him. A short distance away another native was speaking to a crowd in Bantu [an African language]. Called Dutchmen "dumb." Pointed to a picture of Negroes marching in Courier and said: "See here how 10,000 American black men march to show the world that they are equal to any people on earth." Said black men in Africa asleep. Denounced poor whites in South Africa—said they would take all black men's jobs. Attacked the rich. Said rich are sitting on their riches, on the gold and diamonds that rightfully belong to the natives, and that time had come for poor men to demand their share. Said white men had robbed natives of their own gold and diamonds in their own country. But said native is changing. He is oppressed by white man's laws . . . and white man must change them and give him good laws or native is ready to die. Being starved to death anyway.*

---

*Robert R. Edgar, ed., *An African American in South Africa: The Travel Notes of Ralph J. Bunche, 28 September 1937–1 January 1938*. Athens, Ohio: Ohio University Press, 1992, pp. 55-56.

AFRIKANER IDENTITY

Afrikaner resentment was not a new phenomenon. It had been festering ever since the Boer War failed to resolve the tensions between the British and the Boers, from whom Afrikaners were descended. In the twentieth century, Afrikaners increasingly formed a strong sense of identity, created in large part by their hatred of both black South Africans and the British and fostered by the Broederbond (meaning "brotherhood"), an organization founded by teachers and ministers involved in the Dutch Reformed Church. This secretive society believed that God had decreed that Afrikaners should run South Africa. Its members sought to advance the Afrikaner cause politically, socially, and economically.

The Broederbond established the Federasie van Afrikaner Kultuurorganisasies (Federation of Afrikaner Cultural Organizations), also known as the FAK. This organization promoted Afrikaner pride, exhibited art and collected songs that celebrated what Afrikaners saw as their shared culture, and sought to preserve and promote the use of Afrikaans, the language of the Afrikaners. Speaking Afrikaans was a means of distinguishing themselves from English-speaking South Africans of British heritage.

J.B.M. Herzog, the most influential politician of the National Party, championed the Afrikaner cause. He advocated the use of Afrikaans and supported the publication of books in the language. He courted Afrikaners' votes not only by stoking their sense of resentment, but also by rewarding their sense of entitlement. Herzog worked to raise the pay of white workers and espoused the segregationist policies the Afrikaners favored. In 1934, Herzog's National Party merged with the South African Party headed by Jan Smuts. The resulting United Party continued to back the political agenda Herzog developed to court angry Afrikaner voters. Even so, one group of old National Party hard-liners did not think Herzog was doing enough for Afrikaners. Supported by the Broederbond, they formed the more radical Purified National Party.

CELEBRATING THE GREAT TREK

While the government paid increased attention to Afrikaner concerns, the Afrikaner cultural movement was bolstered by the 100-year anniversary of the Great Trek—the migration of Boers from British territory that had led to the establishment of independent Boer republics. Afrikaners commemorated the event by retracing the trek in ox-drawn wagons and reenacting the Battle of Blood River, in which the Boers fought the Zulu. This celebration of the struggles of their Boer ancestors was an emotional experience for Afrikaners. It served to further cement their connection to one another. Dunbar Moodie, a sociologist who studied the Afrikaners in the 1970s, noted that his Afrikaner interview subjects all recalled the 1938 centennial as a deeply important personal experience.

During the 1930s, many Afrikaners watched developments in Germany with an intense interest. Adolf Hitler's Nazi Party had risen to power in 1933 by appealing to disgruntled Germans in many of the same ways the National Party courted the Afrikaners. Specifically, both parties played on their followers' hatred of an oppressed group within their population—the Jews in Germany and elsewhere in Europe, and the black South Africans.

Not surprisingly, many Afrikaners were taken aback when South Africa officially sided with Great Britain against Germany in World War II (1939–1945). They were angry that South Africa was supporting the British, whom they felt were their enemies, instead of the Germans, whose politics and culture they admired. About 250,000 Afrikaners joined the Ossewabrandwag ("Ox-wagon Guard"), a paramilitary group organized by participants in the Great Trek centennial. The most militant members of the organization committed acts of sabotage to protest South Africa's position in the war.

RISING TENSIONS

During the war years, the South African economy rebounded. Industries that served the needs of their military allies boomed, which only increased the flood of workers to towns and cities. The mass migration created a housing crisis in urban areas throughout the country. Black workers had trouble finding places to live. Entire families crowded into tiny apartments. Other workers lived in makeshift shanties on unoccupied plots. These shantytowns often were filthy and crime-ridden.

Within this chaotic atmosphere, blacks new to the city began to band together. They created social organizations to help one another out in times of need. In the cities, a unique culture called marabi emerged, centering on shebeens (beer halls) and a style of music that combined American ragtime and jazz with rural musical traditions. The migration to cities also reinvigorated the labor movement among black workers. During the desperate years of the 1930s, workers were too dispirited to protest, but in the 1940s boom, they once again came together to fight for better living and working conditions. Urban blacks used boycotts and strikes to force the government and their employers to address their demands. In the biggest protest of the era, 70,000 mine workers staged a massive strike in 1946. As it had in the past, the government sent in troops to attack the strikers.

The violence succeeded in squashing the strike, but that was little comfort to many whites. The strike had revived their worst nightmare—that the black majority would one day rise up and seize power from them. That nagging fear was enough to convince both British and Afrikaner South Africans they had to subdue the black population completely before it had a chance to revolt.

4

Apartness

After World War II ended in 1945, the world witnessed a new phenomenon—decolonization. In recent centuries, Great Britain and other European nations had sought control over other peoples and their resources by establishing colonies in Africa and Asia. This process was reversed following the war, largely because the colonies had become too expensive to maintain. The racism and white supremacy of the defeated Nazi regime also helped to accelerate the end of colonialism. The blatant evils of Nazism made it impossible to form a moral case for one country's oppression over another.

Unlike European nations, South Africa did not follow this growing international trend. In fact, it embraced racism in the postwar era as the single guiding principle for structuring its political and economic culture. As a result, South Africa crafted a uniquely and extraordinarily unjust and unstable society.

THE REUNITED NATIONAL PARTY

During the war years (1939–1945), the United Party (UP), led by Jan Smuts, dominated South African politics. Whites of British ancestry and some Afrikaners supported it. But during the late 1940s, many Afrikaners started abandoning the party. They instead shifted their allegiance to the Reunited National Party, which became known simply as the National Party (NP). (This new National Party included members of the Purified National Party and other former members of the old National Party founded in 1914.)

Some NP members, or Nationalists, were disillusioned with Smuts's rule. He supported the British bankers and mine owners whom many Afrikaners felt had too much power over the South African economy. Other Nationalists were attracted to the rhetoric of the NP, which championed the Afrikaner people and their shared culture. Still other Nationalists believed the UP was too liberal in dealing with the black majority. As more and more blacks moved to the cities, these working-class party members feared for their jobs and neighborhoods. They also were alarmed by the mine workers' strike of 1946 and worried that Smuts would cave to the demands of black workers, which would jeopardize the special treatment to which whites had grown accustomed.

TOTAL SEGREGATION

Frightened Afrikaners demanded a plan to preserve white privilege. The NP responded with the Sauer Report. It called for "total segregation" as the government's "eventual ideal and goal."[1] Under the total segregation policy, the only black South Africans who would be allowed in cities were male workers. Their movements would be tracked and controlled by special government bureaus. All black women and children would be confined to designated areas in the countryside.

The UP countered by issuing the Fagan Report. It outlined proposals for dealing with increased urbanization but offered no real changes to its policies concerning black workers. The UP argued that total segregation would be impossible to implement. Furthermore, the party held that it was inevitable that black workers would become a permanent presence in urban areas. For hard-line Nationalists, this argument was infuriating. They falsely claimed that Smuts and his party were calling for the complete integration of the races in South Africa. In their eyes, integration would lead to nothing short of mass violence and chaos.

To avoid this fate, the NP advocated a policy of apartheid, an Afrikaans word meaning "apartness." The Nationalists saw apartheid as a means of completely separating people of different races in all spheres of activity. In their eyes, only through apartheid could the government achieve its ultimate goal: "It is the primary task and calling of the State to seek the welfare of South Africa, and to promote the happiness and well-being of its citizens, non-White as well as White. . . . Such a task can best be accomplished by preserving and safeguarding the White race."[2]

THE ELECTION OF 1948

The 1948 parliamentary election revealed just how compelling the message of the NP was for many Afrikaners. The UP triumphed in the popular vote, but the NP won the most seats in the parliament. By the rules of the South African constitution, the NP therefore controlled the government. Its leader, D.F. Malan, was named the new prime minister.

After taking power, the NP scrambled to put its apartheid policies in place. Its leaders knew they might not have much time. The NP was just popular enough to win a majority of parliamentary seats, but there were no guarantees it would be able to hold on to them come the next election. The party was determined to push through whatever legislation it could while it was still in control.

The UP was also skeptical of the NP's staying power. Smuts publicly predicted the apartheid agenda would fail. He said

Pictured, an apartheid sign in 1953. The system of apartheid kept the races in South Africa completely separated from 1948 to 1994.

apartheid was impractical because the policy made no plans to educate or train black workers. Using the kind of racist language common to members of both parties, Smuts declared, "[The black worker] has to become more efficient, he cannot remain simply a barbarian, working on the lowest level. He must be shaped into an economic instrument; he must be made economically and industrially efficient."[3]

LEGISLATING APARTHEID

Hoping to prove Smuts wrong, the NP quickly pushed through a series of laws that touched on every aspect of the lives of South Africans. They drew on older discriminatory legislation but were more sweeping in their goal to create a racially seg-regated society. Taken together, these laws from the 1950s are often referred to as petty apartheid.

Parliament passed two of the most significant apartheid laws in 1950. One was the Population Registration Act. By its terms, all South Africans were categorized by their race. Initially, the government recognized three categories: White, Colored, and Native (later renamed Bantu). Natives were black South Africans, while Coloreds were people of mixed black and white ancestry. Nine years later, a fourth category—Asian—was added for immigrants from India and their descendants. Everyone in the country was assigned to a category and given an ID card that designated his or her racial classification according to the government.

The second law was the Group Areas Act. It divided the country into geographical areas, each of which was set aside for use by a separate racial category. To regulate the movement of people through these areas, the government passed the Native Laws Amendment Act in 1952. In the past, in many parts of South Africa, black men had to carry special passes to legally enter certain areas. This law extended the pass system through-out the country and made passes mandatory for both women and men. Each black South African received what was called a "reference book," which contained a photograph and personal information. If a black person entered a white area without a reference book, he or she could be sent to jail.

The government also opposed any blurring of racial lines and passed several laws dealing with the most personal aspects of people's lives. To stop the growth of the mixed-race popula-tion, laws banned all marriages and even any sexual contact between people of different races. The Reservation of Separate Amenities Act of 1953 also had a broad impact on South Africans' daily lives. It called for all public elements of social life to be segregated. Whites, Natives, and Coloreds had their own buses, movie theaters, restaurants, sports arenas, and public bathrooms. All over the country, signs appeared designating which race could use certain buildings and facilities. The law further said that these facilities did not have to be of equal quality. Unsurprisingly, those for Whites were far better constructed and maintained than those for Natives and Coloreds.

THE BANTU EDUCATION ACT

Some other significant apartheid laws made labor unions illegal for black South Africans and established rural governments for black South Africans, which were headed by chiefs chosen for their willingness to support the apartheid agenda. But the law that perhaps inflicted the most long-term damage on black South Africans was the Bantu Education Act of 1953. Previously, most black children who received an education went to mission schools run by religious groups. The new law ended all government funding to mission schools, most of which then had to close their doors.

Black children now had no choice but to attend new government-run schools. These schools not only had poor facilities; they also provided an inadequate education. The schools' curricula focused on molding black children into compliant, productive workers who would never question or make demands of their white employers. A schoolteacher named Ezekiel Mphahlele later wrote about how appalled he was by the new textbooks the government provided: "[There is] a history book with several distortions meant to glorify white colonization . . . and white rule; . . . and a literature [text] that teems with non-white characters who are savages or blundering idiots to be despised and laughed at."[4] A second act, passed in 1959, created a segregated university system. Blacks could go to a white institution only if they received special permission from the government.

These educational reforms were the brainchild of H.F. Verwoerd, the minister of native affairs. He believed blacks were inferior and, therefore, a decent education would only

encourage the false hope that they could become the intel-
lectual equals of whites. He declared that the mission schools
had "misled [black South Africans] by showing them the green
pastures of European society in which they are not allowed
to graze."[5] Verwoerd's sentiments were echoed by a 1954
declaration issued by the Dutch Reformed Church. In it, the
church provided whites with a moral justification for apartheid, despite the system's obvious and outrageous injustices:
"Equality between natives, coloureds and Europeans includes a
misappreciation of the fact that God, in His Providence, made
people into different races and nations. . . . Far from the word
of God encouraging equality, it is an established scriptural
principle that in every community ordination there is a fixed
relationship between authorities."[6]

Whites continued to support apartheid in growing num-
bers. Despite the belief of UP members that it did not have
staying power, the NP won reelection in 1953 and 1958, taking
a larger majority of parliamentary seats each time. Because
apartheid succeeded in preserving white privileges, it earned
the respect of ever more Afrikaners. Some British South
Africans, particularly businesspeople, also began supporting
the NP. They were pleased that apartheid had provided them a
steady supply of cheap African laborers.

RESISTING THE APARTHEID REGIME

For black South Africans, of course, apartheid was an utter
disaster. Apartheid laws left them mired in poverty, unable to
get a decent education, and vulnerable to an oppressive government intent on controlling everything they did. It also made
them the victims of a violent police state that persecuted and
imprisoned anyone who defied the country's racist laws.

Despite these threats, many black South Africans risked their
lives to challenge apartheid. Before the 1948 election, the African
National Congress (ANC) was the best-established black political group in South Africa. But when the apartheid system was

An October 1952 photo of Walter Sisulu, Nelson Mandela *(center)*, and Harrison Motlana, three members of the Defiance Campaign through which the African National Congress (ANC) advocated nonviolent protests against apartheid.

put in place, some members felt that the ANC was not aggressive enough. They included the members of an ANC-offshoot, the Congress Youth League (CYL). Founded by Anton Lembede, Ashley Peter Mda, Nelson Mandela, Walter Sisulu, and Oliver Tambo, the CYL pushed the ANC to stage boycotts, strikes, and other forms of civil disobedience. They were inspired by the nonviolent protests of the Indian political and spiritual leader Mahatma Gandhi, who had led the South Africa Indian population in nonviolent protests against the Smuts government in 1906. His method of nonviolent protests eventually convinced the British government to give up its control over India.

In 1949, the CYL leaders announced their goals for the ANC in the Program of Action. The document explained that the CYL wanted to achieve "national freedom from White domination and the attainment of political independence [which] implies the rejection of the conception of segregation, apartheid, trusteeship, or white leadership."[7]

The government responded with a new law, the Suppression of Communism Act of 1950. The act supposedly was directed at members of South Africa's small Communist Party. But the law's definition of *Communist* was so loose it could be applied to any critic of the government. Under the law, political parties could be banned, and suspected Communists could be arrested and detained without charges.

The law only strengthened the resolve of the ANC. Its leaders decided to join forces with the South African Indian Congress (SAIC), a political organization that represented the oppressed Indian minority. Together, the ANC and the SAIC launched the Defiance Campaign in 1952. Hundreds of thousands turned out for their mass protest rallies. By the end of the year, the government had arrested about 8,500 protesters. Still, the protests helped raise more support for the ANC than ever before. In 1952 alone, its membership rose from 7,000 to 100,000.

THE CONGRESS OF THE PEOPLE

Faced with suppression and banning, the ANC decided to join with more groups that opposed apartheid. Members of the ANC believed they could make a greater impression by having as many anti-apartheid activists participating in their protests as possible. But the strategy also had a moral component. The NP argued that apartheid was necessary because people of different races could never work peaceably together. By staging huge multiracial rallies, the ANC wanted to disprove the NP's racist philosophy.

(continues on page 54)

THE FREEDOM CHARTER

Prior to the 1955 Congress of the People, the political groups involved sent committees throughout South Africa. They compiled a list of demands and grievances many South Africans had with their government. These opinions helped shape a document called the Freedom Charter, which envisioned a new, democratic South Africa—one in which people of all races were granted equality and basic human rights. A seminal document of the anti-apartheid movement, it outlined the policies pursued by the ANC for the next 40 years:

We, the People of South Africa, declare for all our country and the world to know:

that South Africa belongs to all who live in it, black and white, and that no government can justly claim authority unless it is based on the will of all the people; . . .

that only a democratic state, based on the will of all the people, can secure to all their birthright without distinction of colour, race, sex or belief;

And therefore, we, the people of South Africa, black and white together equals, countrymen and brothers adopt this Freedom Charter; . . .

The People Shall Govern!

Every man and woman shall have the right to vote for and to stand as a candidate for all bodies which make laws; . . .

All National Groups Shall have Equal Rights!

There shall be equal status in the bodies of state, in the courts and in the schools for all national groups and races; . . .

The People Shall Share in the Country's Wealth!

The national wealth of our country, the heritage of South Africans, shall be restored to the people; . . .

The Land Shall be Shared Among Those Who Work It!

Restrictions of land ownership on a racial basis shall be ended, and all the land re-divided amongst those who work it to banish famine and land hunger; . . .

All Shall be Equal Before the Law!

No-one shall be imprisoned, deported or restricted without a fair trial; . . .

All Shall Enjoy Equal Human Rights!

The law shall guarantee to all their right to speak, to organise, to meet together, to publish, to preach, to worship and to educate their children; . . .

There Shall be Work and Security!

All who work shall be free to form trade unions, to elect their officers and to make wage agreements with their employers; . . .

Men and women of all races shall receive equal pay for equal work; . . .

The Doors of Learning and Culture Shall be Opened!

The government shall discover, develop and encourage national talent for the enhancement of our cultural life; . . .

Education shall be free, compulsory, universal and equal for all children; . . .

There Shall be Houses, Security and Comfort!

All people shall have the right to live where they choose, be decently housed, and to bring up their families in comfort and security; . . .

There Shall be Peace and Friendship!

South Africa shall be a fully independent state which respects the rights and sovereignty of all nations; . . .

Let all people who love their people and their country now say, as we say here:

THESE FREEDOMS WE WILL FIGHT FOR, SIDE BY SIDE, THROUGHOUT OUR LIVES, UNTIL WE HAVE WON OUR LIBERTY*

*Excerpted from The Freedom Charter, African National Congress. http://www.anc.org.za/ancdocs/history/charter.html.

(continued from page 51)

In June 1955, more than 2,000 activists gathered in the township of Soweto for the Congress of the People. In addition to representatives from the ANC and the SAIC, members of the South African Coloured People's Organization and the Congress of Democrats, a political group for white opponents of apartheid, attended the event. At the meeting, the delegates unanimously approved the Freedom Charter. The document presented their vision of South Africa's future. They saw it as a democratic state in which people of all races would be treated as equals. The Freedom Charter was later endorsed by all the member organizations and by the South African Communist Party.

After the publication of the Freedom Charter, the apartheid government passed a censorship law that allowed a board of censors to ban any publications, books, or films that the government found offensive. One of the board's most ridiculous actions was to ban the English novel *Black Beauty* about a horse by that name. The censors did not want to give black South Africans the idea that anything black could also be beautiful.

NEW STRATEGIES

About a year after the Congress of the People, the South African government arrested 156 leaders of the anti-apartheid movement and accused them of having ties with the Communist Party. Thirty were charged with treason and put on trial. The drawn-out trial lasted for nearly five years. Although the South African Supreme Court eventually overturned the case, the trial was a blow to the anti-apartheid movement. It both distracted the movement's leadership and drained the movement of energy and money.

South Africans, however, continued to protest the apartheid regime. One of the most dramatic demonstrations was staged by the ANC-affiliated Federation of South African Women, which was founded in 1954. In 1956, 20,000 of its members

A crowd gathers at the township of Sharpeville, south of Johannesburg, South Africa, on March 21, 1960, a few hours before white police officers opened fire on them.

stormed through the streets of Pretoria to protest the issuing of passes to women.

Even as the anti-apartheid movement grew, some activists were becoming disillusioned with the ANC by the late 1950s. Despite all its efforts, the ANC had demonstrated very little success in changing the South African government. Instead of reconsidering its apartheid agenda, the government had responded to each protest by heightening its suppression of all criticism.

A few more radical ANC members also questioned the group's links with other political organizations. They thought that instead of working with groups of whites and Indians, the

ANC should be fighting to make South Africa a state ruled by blacks. Adopting the slogan "Africa for Africans," these activists broke ties with the ANC to found the Pan-Africanist Congress (PAC) in 1959. The PAC secretly received funding by the U.S. government, which opposed the ANC. U.S. officials thought that the ANC was too closely tied to South African Communists sympathetic to the Soviet Union, which the United States then considered its greatest enemy.

THE SHARPEVILLE MASSACRE

In December 1959, the ANC announced that it would hold a series of one-day protests against the pass laws. The PAC decided to do one better. They organized their own anti-pass campaign. In their protests, demonstrators would leave their passes at home, march to a police station, and demand that they all be arrested.

On March 21, 1960, a group of PAC protesters descended on the police station in Sharpeville, a township near Johannesburg. The march was nonviolent, but the Sharpeville police, worried by the size of the crowd, panicked. From armored cars, the police began shooting at the protesters. At least 69 people were killed and about 180 were wounded. Many were shot in the back as they ran to escape the gunfire. After the massacre, Prime Minister H.F. Verwoerd declared a state of emergency. About 18,000 demonstrators were arrested, and the ANC and PAC were banned.

WITH THE WORLD WATCHING

The Sharpeville Massacre marked a turning point in the struggle against apartheid. In its aftermath, all anti-apartheid leaders were driven underground. Hiding from the police, they began to reconsider their commitment to nonviolent protest. With the slaughter in Sharpeville, nonviolence no longer seemed an effective tool against a brutally ruthless government.

The Sharpeville Massacre also escalated the international criticism of apartheid and of the South African government. The United Nations even considered levying economic sanctions on South Africa. The plan was opposed by Great Britain and the United States, however, because British and American businesses were heavily invested in South African industries. Even so, with the world watching, condemnation of the National Party and its brutal regime was growing. Verwoerd responded with anger. In 1960, the prime minister attended a conference of the nations of the British Commonwealth, of which South Africa, as a former British colony, was then a member. Greeted with harsh criticism at the conference, Verwoerd petulantly proposed that South Africa withdraw from the commonwealth altogether in 1961. His actions made clear that South Africa was determined to follow its own course no matter what. By choice, the nation was becoming ever more isolated from the rest of the world.

5

Fighting Back

In 1961, the year after the Sharpeville Massacre, the National
Party once again won the South African parliamentary election. It now held more than twice the number of seats in the
parliament as its rival, the United Party. Many white South
Africans of British ancestry had shifted their allegiance to the
NP. Although most of them were still put off by the party's celebration of Afrikaner culture, they were pleased by the effect
of apartheid on the national economy. By keeping labor costs
extremely low, the NP had succeeded in luring foreign banks
and business concerns into investing in South Africa, allowing
its economy to thrive.

The outcome of the election also encouraged Prime Minister
H.F. Verwoerd to continue crushing the anti-apartheid movement. He was aided in this endeavor by John Vorster, the

minister of justice, who was an enthusiastic supporter of apartheid and of Afrikaner privilege. During World War II, Vorster had been jailed for his participation in a radical Afrikaner group that committed terrorist acts to protest the government's allegiance with Great Britain.

In 1963, the South African parliament passed the General Laws Amendment Act, which allowed the police to arrest and detain South Africans for 90 days without bringing charges against them. After the 90 days, the police could rearrest and detain them for another 90 days, and could repeat this process indefinitely. Only Vorster, as justice minister, had the authority to release a detained prisoner. The law became a powerful weapon against critics of the Verwoerd government.

NEW TACTICS

Faced with violence and detainment, the leaders of the ANC were compelled to adopt new tactics in their fight against apartheid. Previously, the ANC engaged only in nonviolent protests, but, faced with increased police brutality, they felt they had to meet violence with violence. With the ANC banned by the government, Nelson Mandela, living underground, became the commander in chief of a new, armed wing of the ANC, Umkhonto we Sizwe (meaning "Spear of the Nation"). Umkhonto we Sizwe bombed police stations, power plants, and other government buildings, although its members took precautions to ensure that no one was killed during these attacks.

In 1963, the South African police arrested many leaders of Umkhonto we Sizwe, including Mandela. Those arrested were charged with sabotage. Most were taken into custody at a farmhouse in the suburb of Rivonia near Johannesburg. The lengthy Rivonia trial ended in 1964 with an eloquent four-hour speech delivered by Mandela. He declared that he would rather die than give up the armed struggle against pro-apartheid forces.

Eight defendants, including Mandela, were sent to prison for life. Seven were placed in the prison on Robben Island, which became known for its many political prisoners involved in the anti-apartheid movement. The eighth, a white man, had to be sent to another facility because even the South African prison system was completely segregated.

GRAND APARTHEID

By the mid-1960s, just about all anti-apartheid leaders had been imprisoned or driven underground. At the same time, the movement also suffered from the government's implementa- tion of grand apartheid. The goal of grand apartheid was to so separate the races that whites seldom even encountered blacks unless the blacks worked for them. In patronizing language, Prime Minister Verwoerd explained in a speech to black South Africans how this plan would allow each race to "develop" according to its natural strengths and abilities:

> Separate development is a tree, a fruit tree which this Government gave the Bantu [blacks] of South Africa. It planted the tree, but that tree must be tended in order to grow.... Let it grow slowly. Do not be impatient. Let the branches become strong so that they can bear many fruits ... do not look at the more developed tree of the white man with jealous eyes because then you will neglect your own small tree which will one day also be big.[1]

CREATING HOMELANDS

The centerpiece of grand apartheid policy was the establish- ment of "homelands" for the nation's black population. In 1959, Verwoerd carved 8 homelands (later increased to 10) out of the reserve lands originally set aside for blacks by the Natives Land Act of 1913. The homelands were not discrete regions with clear-cut borders. Instead, each was a collection of scattered tracts of poor-quality land. One homeland, KwaZulu, was made up of some 70 different tracts.

Theoretically, the homelands were supposed to correspond to old territories traditionally controlled by different tribes. In fact, the populations assigned to the different homelands did not have such shared tribal identities. This was a myth spread by the government to suggest that blacks were returning to their "natural" state of being, before their lives were disrupted by urbanization.

Black South Africans did not move to the homelands voluntarily. Most were forcibly removed from townships. They were able to bring with them only the few possessions they could carry. Often, bulldozers destroyed their old homes and neighborhoods. Between the mid-1950s and the mid-1980s, about 3.5 million blacks were relocated to the homelands. This massive forced migration was casually referred to as "erasing black spots"[2] by officials of the apartheid government.

South Africans removed to the homelands had to struggle to rebuild their lives. The living conditions were generally very poor. Homeland residents often had little access to hospitals, electricity sources, or even supplies of clean water. As more and more people were removed, the homelands also became extremely overcrowded. For most of the day, poor women and children were left alone in the homelands, because men had to work in urban areas to support their families. Commuting laborers often had to travel more than 100 miles (160 kilometers) to their jobs. Each morning and evening, they spent many hours on rickety buses that transported them from their homelands to the cities and then back again.

WORKERS AND STUDENTS

During the 1960s, the anti-apartheid movement seemed stalled in its tracks. The government had effectively silenced its most vocal critics. In addition, the homelands policy had helped to end organized resistance, because black South Africans were too consumed with the struggles of day-to-day life to fight against apartheid policy. The then-thriving South African economy, buoyed by foreign investment, also convinced many whites to support NP policies no matter how unjust or immoral they were.

Yet by the early 1970s, it was becoming clear that apartheid was both socially and economically unsustainable. Black employees were too poor to buy many of the goods produced by South African companies, limiting the companies profits and growth; and with black workers forbidden to organize unions, employers and employees also had no legal means of solving labor disputes, which made businesses vulnerable to illegal strikes.

South Africa's education policies also produced unintended results. Petty apartheid had greatly reduced the educational opportunities of blacks. They could only attend segregated schools, where the curriculum had been designed to mold them into submissive workers who would do whatever their employers said. In practice, however, black students easily saw through the government's attempt to brainwash them into believing they were inferior to whites. Instead of producing passive laborers, the education system created a new generation of angry young activists eager to stand up against the government and its condescending dismissal of their intelligence and talents.

THE WILDCAT STRIKES OF 1973

In January 1973, bricklayers in Durban, a leading industrial center, walked off the job. They were fed up with their low wages, which could not keep up with the rising prices of goods caused by a downturn in the economy. It was a wildcat strike—that is, a strike organized by workers without the support or authorization of a union. The bricklayers were so desperate that they felt they had nothing to lose by fighting back against their employers.

As news of the strike spread, other laborers decided to follow the example. Spontaneously, workers staged strikes all over Durban and beyond. Within three months, there were 160 different strike actions across South Africa, involving about 60,000 workers. The police, caught off guard and overwhelmed, were unsure about what to do to end the strikes. The strikers were careful not to identify who their leaders were. As a result, the police had no idea whom to arrest.

In the past, the employers would have simply fired the strikers and hired new workers to take their place. But now South Africa's economy had shifted away from farming and mining and toward manufacturing. Manufacturers needed trained, experienced factory workers, so the striking employees could not be replaced so easily. The factory owners desperately wanted to get their businesses back up and running, but the apartheid policies that outlawed unions made that nearly impossible. Without any worker representatives to negotiate with, employers did not know how to get their employees back to work.

Under pressure from employers and employees alike, the parliament passed the Bantu Labour Relations Regulation Amendment Act, which gave black workers the right to strike and allowed them to elect committees to represent them during labor disputes. The law marked a victory for the long-dormant anti-apartheid movement. It also showed black workers how important they were to the South African economy. That knowledge, in turn, gave them a new sense of confidence about what they could accomplish if they all worked together.

BIKO AND BLACK CONSCIOUSNESS

While workers were discovering their power to enact change, students were inspired by news of black activism in the United States. In the late 1960s and early 1970s, the Black Power movement tried to foster a new racial pride in African Americans,

(continues on page 66)

A photo of Stephen Biko, the South African anti-apartheid activist who died in police custody in 1977.

STEPHEN BIKO

Stephen Biko was born on December 18, 1946, in King William's Town. Encouraged by his father, Biko was determined to get a good education. During his youth, however, the government passed the Bantu Education Act, which limited the educational opportunities available to black South Africans. Angered by these restrictions, Biko became further embittered after the police, suspecting he was a political activist, interrogated him. He was subsequently expelled from school.

Biko eventually was able to attend the University of Natal to study medicine. While a student there, he became more involved in the anti-apartheid movement. Biko joined the National Union of South African Students (NUSAS), but he grew disillusioned with the group because its white leaders did not show enough interest in the problems of black students. Biko left the NUSAS to establish the South African Students' Organization (SASO), an all-black student group, in 1968.

With Biko as its leader, the SASO promoted the doctrine of Black Consciousness, which held that black South Africans had been taught to hate themselves and to view whites as their superiors. They could only enact real social and political change if they first developed a sense of pride in their identity as black people. Biko felt that whites should not be part of the fight against apartheid. He believed that blacks had to spearhead their own liberation from the white-dominated power structure in South Africa.

As the Black Consciousness movement grew, the government tried to silence Biko. He was prohibited from making

(continues)

(continued)

public speeches and attending school. Biko's influence, however, was still felt by student activists, especially those involved in the Soweto riots of 1976. With black students throughout South Africa rebelling, the government respond- ed with a police crackdown. Biko was detained for 101 days, and then released without being charged with a crime. He was again taken into police custody on August 18, 1977. He died on September 12 after receiving a blow to the head while in detention.

Thousands of mourners tried to attend Biko's funeral, but police armed with rifles and machine guns stopped many at roadblocks. Despite the police's efforts, Biko's funeral turned into a political rally. At his burial site, a massive crowd gath- ered. As his coffin was lowered into the crowd, mourners thrusted their fists in the air and shouted, "Power!"

Biko's death also received attention from international critics of apartheid, who called for a complete investiga- tion into his cause of death. The police tried to cover up his murder, first claiming he had died as the result of a hunger strike, and then attributing his death to an accident. In 1997, the Truth and Reconciliation Commission finally uncov- ered the circumstances of his murder. In South Africa, the life and work of Stephen Biko is still celebrated each year on the anniversary of his death.

(continued from page 63)

who had long been subjected to legal discrimination in the United States. The movement also advocated the creation of cultural and political institutions that would promote African Americans' interests and their quest for equal rights.

On black college campuses in South Africa, these ideas created a new philosophy called Black Consciousness. Its main proponent was Stephen Biko, who founded the South African Students' Organization (SASO) in 1969. Biko held that, because of years of oppression, black South Africans had been taught to hate themselves. They had internalized the message that they were inferior to whites. Biko believed that only after they had learned to accept and respect their black identity would black South Africans be successful in their fight for their rights: "Blacks are suffering from an inferiority complex—a result of 300 years of deliberate oppression, denigration and derision. . . . What is necessary . . . is a very strong grass-roots build-up of black consciousness such that blacks can learn to assert themselves and stake their rightful claim."[3]

In Biko's eyes, "black" was not a racial category. Instead, it represented anyone in South Africa who had been oppressed by the white minority. Using this definition, he invited everyone the government labeled as Colored and Asian to join the Black Consciousness movement. Biko, however, did not want whites involved with his cause. He claimed that even the most well-meaning whites had been tainted by the idea that they were superior to and smarter than blacks. If whites wanted to end apartheid, he felt they should concentrate on changing the minds of other whites instead of joining black South Africans in their fight for justice.

SOWETO

At first, South African officials did not oppose Biko's movement. Because he rejected white involvement, they saw Black Consciousness as being in synch with their program of racial segregation. But it was soon clear that Biko's SASO was a formidable force in a revitalized anti-apartheid movement. In 1972, when the SASO organized massive class boycotts on black universities, the government responded by arresting more than 600 students.

In 1974, the Ministry of Bantu Education decided to enforce a legal requirement that the Afrikaans language be used

Antoinette Sithole, sister of Hector Pieterson who was murdered by South African police, poses alongside the iconic photograph taken by Sam Nzima at the Hector Pieterson Memorial in Soweto.

in schools. The decision angered many school administrators. They did not have enough Afrikaans textbooks or Afrikaans-speaking teachers to comply. It also infuriated black students. Many young black South Africans, especially those involved in the Black Consciousness movement, considered Afrikaans the language of their oppressors and therefore were offended by the ministry's demands.

To protest the new rule, the SASO organized hundreds of grammar and secondary school students in Soweto, a township outside of Johannesburg. Boycotting their classes, they peacefully marched to a large soccer stadium for a mass protest on June 16, 1976. At about nine o'clock in the morning, the

"THEY SIMPLY OPENED FIRE"

In his best-selling memoir *Kaffir Boy* (1986), Mark Mathabane recounted his youth in South Africa. Like other black South Africans in the 1960s and 1970s, he had to endure the humiliations and brutality of life under the apartheid system. In this excerpt from his memoirs, Mathabane describes the fear and hatred he felt as a 15-year-old boy when he learned of the massacre of students in Soweto in 1976:

No one thought it would happen, yet everyone knew it had to happen. All the hate, bitterness, frustration and anger that had crystallized into a powder keg in the minds of black students, waiting for a single igniting spark, found that spark when the Department of Bantu Education suddenly decreed that all black schools had to teach courses in Afrikaans instead of English.

The first spontaneous explosion took place in Soweto on the afternoon of Wednesday, June 16, 1976, where about ten thousand students marched through the dirt streets of Soweto protesting the Afrikaans decree. . . .

Unknown to the marchers, . . . hundreds of policemen, armed with tear gas canisters, rifles, shotguns and *sjamboks* [whips with metal tips], had formed a barricade across the street. . . .

While student leaders argued about what to do to diffuse the situation, the police suddenly opened fire. Momentarily the crowd stood dazed, thinking that the bullets were plastic and had been fired into the air. But when several small children began dropping down like swatted flies, their white uniforms soaked in red blood, pandemonium broke out.

The police continued firing into the crowd. Students fled into houses alongside the street; others tripped, fell

(continues)

(continued)

and were trampled underfoot. Some were so shocked they didn't know what to do except scream and cry. Still others fought bullets with rocks and schoolbags. . . .

In the school bus from Tembisa, reading the gruesome accounts of what took place in Soweto in the late after-noon edition of the *World*, I felt hate and anger well up inside me. . . .

The bus was packed, yet silent. Heads were buried inside newspapers. Tears flowed freely down the cheeks of youths returning from school, and men and women returning from work. I again looked at the photo of the two boys, and then and there I knew that my life would never, could never, be the same again.

"They opened fire," mumbled David, who was sit-ting alongside me, shaking his head with disbelief. "They didn't give any warning. They simply opened fire. Just like that. Just like that," he repeated. "And small chil-dren, small defenseless children, dropped down like swat-ted flies. This is murder, cold-blooded murder."

There was nothing I could say in reply, except stare back. No words could possibly express what I felt. No words could express the hatred I felt for the white race.

"This is the beginning of something too ugly to con-template," David said. "Our lives can, and should, never be the same after this."

I nodded.*

---

*Mark Mathabane, *Kaffir Boy: The True Story of a Black Youth's Coming of Age in Apartheid South Africa*. New York: Simon & Schuster, 1986, pp. 259-260.

police arrived. They quickly panicked and began throwing tear gas and shooting into the crowd. Many students were killed, including 13-year-old Hector Pieterson. A horrifying news photograph of the boy's body being carried by a friend was published in papers around the world.

A MARTYR'S DEATH

The Soweto massacre set off a wave of violence. Throughout South Africa, angry students burned down government buildings and beer halls, which led to more confrontations with the police. By the end of 1976, nearly 600 protesters had been killed. Tens of thousands were detained. Many were tortured in jail.

Among those arrested after Soweto was Stephen Biko. On September 12, 1977, while in police custody, the student leader died of massive head injuries. The police's official explanation held that Biko was responsible for his own death. He supposedly became aggressive, throwing a chair and punching his interrogators, before accidentally hitting his head on a wall as they frantically tried to subdue him. Years later, the police admitted the truth: He had been tortured to death during interrogation. In the end, Biko's killing only served to steel the resolve of a new generation of South Africans, inspiring them to continue the fight against apartheid no matter what the cost.

Reform and Repression

The tumultuous reign of John Vorster, the prime minister since 1966, came to an end in 1978 when a financial scandal drove him from office. He was replaced by P.W. Botha, a familiar face in South African politics. He was not only a dedicated supporter of the National Party, but also had served as defense minister since 1966.

Botha's first priority after becoming prime minister was to restore the business community's confidence in the government. Many business owners and investors were unsettled by the violence of the Soweto massacre and its aftermath. They worried that South African society was unstable, its workforce too volatile. In addition, South Africa now had to deal with unfriendly neighboring countries. In 1975, Mozambique and Angola had won their independence from Portugal. Their new black-dominated governments allowed the ANC's armed wing, the Umkhonto we Sizwe, to establish camps within their borders. These camps trained young men, many of whom escaped from South Africa after Soweto, to engage in armed guerrilla warfare against the South African government.

THE TOTAL STRATEGY

Faced with social chaos, hostile neighbor nations, and shaky economic conditions, Botha adopted what he called the Total Strategy. As part of this plan, the prime minister proposed a number of reforms to help placate the black population. Botha cautioned his white supporters that these reforms were necessary if the NP-controlled government were to stay in power. He told South Africa's white population that it had only two choices: "adapt or die."[1]

Many of Botha's reforms removed minor, though hated, restrictions placed on blacks through apartheid legislation. For instance, he ended the regulations against interracial marriages, desegregated some public facilities, increased funds for black schools, and loosened the rules forbidding blacks from living in urban areas. But his most significant reforms involved workers' rights. In 1977, the government had established the Wiehahn Commission to study ways to improve the South African workforce. The commission's report, released two years later, noted that the white population was dropping. Because there were not enough whites to fill all the highly skilled jobs available, blacks had to be trained to take these posts. It also cited that workers needed legally recognized representatives to help negotiate labor disputes with employers. Taking the Wiehahn Commission's recommendations, Botha's government removed the "color bars" that prohibited blacks from holding certain well-paying skilled jobs. Even more importantly, it lifted the ban on unions for black workers. Black South Africans now could form legal unions to air their grievances over unacceptable working conditions.

In an effort to calm foreign critics of apartheid, Botha also continued a policy inaugurated by Prime Minister H.F. Verwoerd. Botha worked to grant "independence" to several of the black-populated homelands. Between 1976 and 1981, the South African government declared that four homelands— Transkei, Bophuthatswana, Venda, and Ciskei—were now independent nations. In fact, these homelands were ruled by puppets of the South African government, who reigned with an iron fist and without any regard for the rule of law. Homeland residents had no illusion about their so-called independence. They knew they still were controlled by the oppressive pro-apartheid regime. The rest of the world also saw through South Africa's ploy. No other country officially recognized any home-land as an independent state.

ATTACKING GOVERNMENT CRITICS

Botha's Total Strategy also included a commitment to using greater force than ever to discourage and punish critics of the government. With his close ties to the army, Botha increasingly relied on soldiers, in addition to police, to suppress the anti-apartheid movement. During his tenure, he doubled the size of the army to ensure he had enough force to attack any group that threatened the apartheid agenda.

Botha not only increased public repression of apartheid protesters, he also secretly initiated violence against anti-apartheid activists living both in South Africa and abroad. During this period, his government's security forces staged a series of assassination attempts, including three unsuccess-ful attacks on Chris Hani, the leader of the South African Communist Party. Their most prominent victim was Ruth First, a longtime critic of apartheid. On August 17, 1982, First was killed by a letter bomb at her office at Eduardo Mondlane University in Mozambique. The South African government also secretly aided groups fighting black-controlled gov-ernments of neighboring states. In addition, South Africa's

MPILO DESMOND TUTU

Born in 1931, Mpilo Desmond Tutu grew up in the mining town of Klerksdorp. He was educated at mission schools, where his father was a teacher. Tutu hoped to become a doctor but could not afford medical school. He instead became a teacher, although three years into his career he quit in protest over the Bantu Education Act of 1953, which severely limited the educational opportunities available for black South Africans. Tutu

Bishop Desmond Tutu, photographed in 1981 at the House of Commons in London.

then attended a theological seminary and was ordained as a priest in the Anglican Church in 1961. After further study in London, England, he became the first black dean of St. Mary's Cathedral in Johannesburg in 1975.

By the late 1970s, Tutu was a leading voice in the struggle against apartheid. At the funeral of activist Stephen Biko in 1977, he declared his belief in the movement: "Nothing, not even the most sophisticated weapon, not even the most brutally efficient police . . . will stop people once they are determined to achieve their freedom and their right to humanness."* The following year, Tutu was named the general secretary of the South African Council of Churches (SACC).

(continues)

(continued)

In this position, he pushed other nations to place economic sanctions on the South African government. He criticized President Ronald Reagan of the United States and British Prime Minister Margaret Thatcher of Great Britain for refusing to support sanctions. He also spoke before the United Nations General Assembly regarding the necessity of ending apartheid. As Tutu explained, "Apartheid cannot be reformed. It must be dismantled. You don't reform a Frankenstein—you destroy it."** Because of his international reputation as a champion for nonviolent opposition to South Africa's unjust policies, Tutu was awarded the Nobel Peace Prize in 1984.

In 1985, Tutu became Johannesburg's Anglican bishop; in 1986, he was named archbishop of Cape Town. He was the first black clergyman to hold these positions. Tutu's continuing outspokenness against apartheid earned him the ill will of Prime Minister P.W. Botha, who approved a campaign of distributing anti-Tutu literature to discredit the archbishop. In 1988, the SACC office was destroyed in a bombing, and Tutu was rumored to be a target for assassination.

After the installation of the first anti-apartheid government, President Nelson Mandela appointed Tutu to serve as the chair of the Truth and Reconciliation Commission. The commission heard testimony from about 22,000 victims of police brutality and other abuses during the apartheid era.

The recipient of many awards and honorary degrees, Tutu was given the Albert Schweitzer Prize for Humanitarianism in 1986 and the International Gandhi Peace Prize in 2007. He continues to be involved with many human rights causes, including alleviating poverty in the Third World, providing medicines to AIDS patients, and fighting discrimination against homosexuals within the Anglican Church.

---

*Lindsay Michie Eades, *The End of Apartheid in South Africa*. Westport, Conn.: Greenwood Press, 1999, p. 151.
**Ibid., p. 152.

security forces raided ANC bases established in Lesotho, Swaziland, Zimbabwe, Botswana, and Mozambique.

By the early 1980s, it became clear that Botha's Total Strategy was far from a success. With a few reforms and increased repression, he had hoped to quiet the government's critics among the black population. But both efforts failed. The more Botha offered angry black South Africans token reforms, the more they demanded a complete rejection of apartheid. The police crackdown on protesters similarly backfired. Rather than frighten government critics into submission, it only stirred their resolve to continue to fight apartheid, and they increasingly met violence with violence. In 1983 alone, the ANC staged 42 attacks on government buildings.

THE CONSTITUTION OF 1983

That same year, Botha unveiled a new national constitution that changed the structure of the government. The national government now would consist of a president, replacing the prime minister's position, and a tricameral (three-part) parliament. The largest parliamentary body represented whites. The two smaller ones represented Asians and Coloreds. Blacks were to be ruled by the homeland governments.

Seemingly no one embraced Botha's tricameral parliament. Blacks were infuriated that Botha created an entirely new constitution that still completely excluded them from representation in the South African government. Asians and Coloreds were angry that the plan offered them no real power. The larger white parliament could outvote the other representatives on any legislation, which rendered the Asians' and Coloreds' role in the new government essentially meaningless.

Many whites in Botha's own party also were appalled by the changes in parliament. They opposed any measure that even suggested Asians and Coloreds should have a say in national legislation. To them, this concession to non-whites—however worthless in real terms—was an unforgivable outrage. It was enough to make a group of hard-liners, led by Andries Treurnicht, leave the NP and form the new Conservative Party.

THE UDF AND COSATU

The tricameral parliament debacle also spurred on disgruntled blacks to form the United Democratic Front (UDF). It was made up of more than 500 community groups that were opposed to Botha's constitutional reforms. The UDF called on all Asians and Coloreds to boycott the election to choose their parliamentary representatives. The boycott was a great success. Only one-third of qualified Asians and Coloreds showed up to vote.

Closely allied to the UDF was the Congress of South African Trade Unions (COSATU). This umbrella organization included members of the dozens of black trade unions that had sprung up. By 1984, more than 500,000 black workers were represented by COSATU. With the organizational powers of the UDF and COSATU, black South Africans mounted some of the largest protests their nation had ever seen. In 1984, protesters in the townships rose up against rising rents and charges for electricity. Students boycotted classes and took to the streets to protest the inferior education they were offered.

During demonstrations, protesters cried out "Viva!" and raised their fists in the air—gestures meant to show their unity with the still-banned ANC. They sang the ANC anthem "Nkosi Sikelel' iAfrika" ("God Bless Africa") and performed the *toyi-toyi*, a defiant dance created in the guerrilla camps of Zimbabwe. Hundreds turned out for the funerals of activists who had died at the hands of the police and the army. Jailed ANC leader Nelson Mandela was hailed as a hero, and Oliver Tambo, an ANC leader who had escaped from South Africa, met with foreign leaders and forged diplomatic ties with other countries. Many of these countries came to regard the ANC as the legitimate government of South Africa.

POLICE BRUTALITY AND VIOLENT PROTEST

Faced with ever-increasing police brutality, the protests of the mid-1980s often turned violent. Protesters sometimes burned down police stations and other official buildings that symbolized the Botha government. They frequently turned their wrath on black police or other black officials who were seen as collaborators with the apartheid regime. In the homelands, young people began to police other residents to make sure they complied with boycotts. In one instance, a woman who bought beer during a boycott of beer halls was forced to drink detergent as a punishment and died the following day. The most gruesome punishment doled out to accused collaborators was called "necklacing," in which a tire filled with gasoline was placed around the collaborator's chest and arms and set on fire.

By the beginning of 1985, Botha was desperate to put an end to the protests. He sent officials to offer Mandela a deal—he would be set free if he agreed to speak out against the escalating violence. The South African government thought that only a man of Mandela's stature could persuade black South Africans to end their protests. By that time, Mandela had spent 21 years behind bars, but he refused the offer without hesitation. He instructed his daughter to read a statement at a UDF rally in Soweto. To a massive crowd, she read his own words describing why he had chosen to reject the chance of freedom:

> What freedom am I being offered while the organization of the people remains banned? What freedom am I being offered when I may be arrested on a pass offence? . . . What freedom am I being offered when I must ask for permission to live in an urban area? . . . What freedom am I being offered when my very South African citizenship is not respected?[2]

A STATE OF EMERGENCY

On March 21, 1985, the police fired on a funeral procession marching through the town of Uitenhage. The funeral was

In the 1980s, the efforts to end apartheid went international. Here, a San Francisco–based group called the Campaign Against Apartheid attempted to prevent the unloading of the South African cargo ship *Nedlloyd Kembla*.

held on the twenty-fifth anniversary of the Sharpeville Massacre, making the police action all the more symbolic. The event led to a string of deadly necklacings of blacks who were known to be working with the Botha regime. In response to the violence on all sides, Minister of Law and Order Adriaan Vlok declared that South Africa was "at the edge of anarchy and bloody revolution."[3]

Botha responded by proclaiming a state of emergency on July 21, 1985. It was the first such measure since the murders at Sharpeville. Under the state of emergency, police were allowed to arrest people without charging them, and the press was forbidden from reporting on the repression of the anti-apartheid movement. As police and soldiers flooded into the townships, protesters were shot at and beaten with sjamboks. Thousands of people were detained, including many members of the UDF. During interrogations, prisoners were routinely tortured. In 1985 alone, the South African police killed more than 500 people.

Despite the government's efforts to censor descriptions and images of police brutality, the violence was widely reported around the globe. Just as the Botha government feared, foreign investors and banks started pulling money out of South Africa, because they worried the social and political chaos was placing their investments at risk. In 1984 and 1985, about 90 American corporations stopped doing business in South Africa, and the biggest U.S. banks refused to make any further loans there. As international investors turned their backs on the country, the nation's currency, the rand, plunged in value.

THE INTERNATIONAL RESPONSE

The violence in South Africa not only troubled the international financial community; it also stirred a sense of moral outrage in people around the world. In the United States, concerned citizens denounced apartheid and pushed for U.S. companies to remove, or divest, all their funds in South Africa as a means of pressuring the government there to reform. College students especially embraced the divestment movement, while many church groups, especially in the African-American community, lent their support to the anti-apartheid cause.

By the mid-1980s, many artists, writers, and popular performers were active in the fight against apartheid. For instance, the critiques of the government by South African authors such as Alan Paton, Nadine Gordimer, and Mark Mathabane were widely read around the world. In the United States, musician

Steven Van Zandt launched a high profile anti-apartheid campaign. He spoke out against performers who agreed to appear at a large luxury resort in South Africa called Sun City. Van Zandt saw their willingness to play this venue as an implicit approval of the apartheid regime. Gathering a lineup of superstar recording artists, including Miles Davis, Bruce Springsteen, and Bob Dylan, Van Zandt recorded the pop song "Sun City." Banned in South Africa, the song spread awareness in the United States of the oppression of black South Africans.

Many governments also applied pressure on Botha's government by placing sanctions on South Africa. For instance, in 1986, the U.S. Congress overrode President Ronald Reagan's veto in order to pass legislation that prohibited any new U.S. investments in and bank loans to South Africa. The law also ended all air travel between the United States and South Africa. The express purpose of these sanctions was to help cripple the South African economy in order to force the government to end its policy of apartheid.

NO END IN SIGHT

In the late 1980s, the sanctions were taking a toll on South Africa. But the deteriorating situation only led both sides to dig in harder. In the anti-apartheid struggle, the UDF organized massive rent strikes and, on the twelfth anniversary of the Soweto killings, COSATU initiated the largest strike in the history of South Africa. An amazing 70 percent of all workers in manufacturing participated. The ANC also stepped up its campaign of armed resistance. Guerrillas trained in foreign ANC bases entered South Africa and began bombing any buildings—from police stations to bars and restaurants—where security forces were known to gather. Pro-apartheid government officials only escalated the violence. Their security forces bombed the headquarters of COSATU and the South African Council of Churches (SACC). They also secretly funded the Inkatha movement, which strongly opposed the ANC and supported the government's policies concerning homelands.

When Botha came to power, he assumed that modest reforms and increased repression would be the answer to South Africa's problems. But by the end of the 1980s, it was clear his policies only had deepened the gulf between the black majority and the white minority. The only common ground they shared was their growing horror over what their country had become. The seemingly unending cycle of violence was tearing South Africa apart as the rest of the world looked on, stunned by revulsion and hopelessness.

Mandela and
de Klerk

At the end of the 1980s, South Africa was trapped in a nightmare scenario. The government, ruled by the white minority, steadfastly refused to make real reforms to eliminate apartheid. At the same time, the black majority refused to end its protests against apartheid, no matter how much violence the protesters were forced to endure at the hands of the police and the army. With both sides unwilling to back down, it looked as though the nation was on the verge of complete chaos.

The stalemate was broken in 1989. In January, President Botha suffered a mild stroke. He resigned his position as head of the National Party and was replaced by F.W. de Klerk. A vocal critic of Botha, de Klerk made it clear that he had his eye on the South African presidency. In August, upset over a slight by rival politicians, Botha abruptly resigned the presidency, which allowed de Klerk to become the nation's new president.

DE KLERK'S REFORMS

De Klerk soon revealed that his rule would represent a clean break from the policies of the past. In his opening remarks to the parliament on February 2, 1990, he made a series of dramatic announcements. De Klerk said that he was lifting the ban on 34 political organizations, including the ANC and the PAC. He also promised to release political prisoners, including Nelson Mandela. These actions would be just the beginning of his reforms. De Klerk resolved to end apartheid and mold South Africa into a modern democratic nation.

Even with these promises, the violence continued. In March 1990, a month after Mandela's release and a few days before the first meeting between the ANC and de Klerk's government, police fired into a crowd of ANC protesters in the township of Sebokeng. Eleven people were killed. Following further protests against the Sebokeng killings, Mandela and de Klerk signed the Groote Schuur Minute in May. In this historic document, the South African government and the ANC finally pledged to put a stop to political violence and to negotiate a peaceful resolution to their disputes.

As the head of the ANC, Mandela was placed under enormous pressure. But his calm composure assured his supporters and convinced some of his initial detractors that he was just the type of confident, competent leader needed to help move the country forward. Knowing he had to exude moral authority in his dealings with the government, Mandela moved his wife, Winnie, to the sidelines of the ANC because she had become a controversial figure during his incarceration by endorsing violence, especially the necklacing of political opponents. In 1991, she was convicted of kidnapping in connection with her

South African President F.W. de Klerk gives a public address in 1992. A year later he shared the Nobel Peace Prize with Nelson Mandela for their efforts in helping to dismantle the apartheid system in South Africa.

bodyguard's murder of James Seipei, a 14-year-old ANC activist suspected of being a police informant. Mandela separated from his wife in 1992. They divorced in 1996.

THE CONSTITUTIONAL CONVENTION

As part of its reform agenda, de Klerk's government agreed to the drafting of a new interim constitution, which would stay in effect until the next popular election. In December 1991, representatives, mostly from the NP and the ANC, came together at the Convention for a Democratic South Africa (CODESA). As the two sides hashed out the terms of the constitution, they had difficulty trusting each other. Mandela especially had his doubts about de Klerk's sincerity. In public, de Klerk asserted that the apartheid era had come to an end. But Mandela felt that de Klerk still held out hope that, in the new South Africa, whites would be given special privileges. In his autobiography, Mandela wrote, "[De Klerk] did not make any of his reforms with the intention of putting himself out of power. He made them for necessarily the opposite reason: to ensure power for the Afrikaner in a new dispensation. He was not yet prepared to negotiate the end of white rule."[1]

The ANC was particularly suspicious about the de Klerk government's ties to the Inkatha Freedom Party (IFP), which grew out of the Inkatha movement. The IFP was behind much of the violence directed against ANC members. Many people believed that the South African government was funding their efforts in order to weaken the ANC and its support. On June 17, 1992, Inkatha supporters entered the township of Boipatong, a stronghold of the ANC, and slaughtered 46 people, most of whom were women and children. The massacre outraged the ANC, especially after the government's security forces made little effort to find those responsible. Calling the killings "the last straw,"[2] Mandela withdrew from the CODESA negotiations with the South African government. The ANC also called a 48-hour national strike, which brought the South African economy to a complete standstill for two days.

On September 7, an ANC protest march in the Ciskei homeland also ended in a massacre. As 80,000 protesters, headed by South African Communist Party leader Chris Hani, entered the homeland's capital, Ciskei security forces opened fire, killing 28 ANC members. Desperate to end the killing, Mandela and de Klerk returned to the negotiating table. The result was the Record of Understanding, in which they agreed to resume talks. De Klerk also finally agreed to hold an election, in which all South Africans—black and white—would be permitted to vote.

THE END OF WHITE RULE

The agreement at last convinced white South Africans that the days of white rule truly were coming to an end. To protect

Pictured, a young girl negotiates a river of water and waste in Duncan Village Township in 1992. Even as apartheid was coming to an end, its impact would be felt for years to come.

themselves, many officials frantically began destroying government documents. They were terrified of prosecution if the extent of unlawful police and military actions ever came to light. They also wanted to destroy documents pertaining to the anti-apartheid movement to keep its long history from being glorified in a black-dominated political climate.

Mandela and de Klerk's agreement also frightened militant groups afraid of losing out in post-apartheid South Africa. Black militants associated with the Inkatha movement continued their terrorist activities. Extreme right-wing Afrikaner groups also vowed to meet the upcoming changes in government with violence. Among them was the Afrikaner Weerstandbeweging (Afrikaner Resistance Movement), known as the AWB. AWB members wore uniforms emblazoned with emblems resembling swastikas to show their admiration for the Nazi Party of Germany.

The AWB tried to intimidate negotiators, storming the hall where their talks were taking place. The group was also responsible for the assassination of Chris Hani at his home in Johannesburg on April 10, 1993. After Hani's murder, Mandela appeared on national television and asked the citizens of South Africa to remain calm and refrain from answering the violence with violence.

At the end of the month, the ANC was demanding that an election date be set. Both sides committed to holding elections one year later, in April 1994. Instead of selecting individual candidates, voters would choose a party, thereby casting their vote for its entire slate of candidates. After the popular election, the members of parliament would vote to select the president.

THE BOPHUTHATSWANA DISASTER

As the election neared, opposition political groups grew more and more frantic. Some, such as the Conservative Party and the Inkatha Freedom Party, declared they would boycott the election. The AWB's rhetoric was even more heated. It vowed to stage a coup to establish an all-white Afrikaner homeland.

In March 1994, the homeland of Bophuthatswana was in chaos. The residents were rising up to oppose Lucas Mangope, the leader of the homeland government who said he would refuse to allow Bophuthatswana to be integrated into a post-apartheid South Africa. Adding to the tensions, Eugene Terreblanche, leader of the AWB, decided to stage a raid on Bophuthatswana with 600 soldiers. On March 10, AWB troops in cars began firing on passersby along the roadside. The Bophuthatswana security forces were appalled by the random murders. At a road-block, television crews and photojournalists caught on camera an incident involving three wounded white AWB members. As they were approached by an armed black soldier, they frantically begged for their lives. He ignored their pleas and gunned the three men down.

The brutal killings caught on film sent a powerful message to white South Africans. The images they saw wiped away any fantasies they had that white rule would survive without violent repercussions. After the Bophuthatswana catastrophe, the AWB lost most of its support. The groups who had planned to boycott the election reconsidered their stance. In the end, they decided that some voice in the new government would be better than no voice at all.

THE ELECTION OF 1994

On April 27, 1994, South Africa held its first truly democratic election. There were a few violent incidents propagated by AWB and Inkatha supporters meant to disrupt the voting. But overall, the election was fairly peaceful. Monitors reported very few instances of voter fraud or intimidation. More than 19 million South Africans voted, amounting to about 90 percent of registered voters. The number included many millions of black citizens who were allowed to vote for the first time. Some had to walk several miles just to get to their polling stations.

Voters wait in line to cast their ballots on day two of South Africa's first democratic elections, held in April 1994.

As expected, the ANC won a huge victory because it was the choice of most black voters. The ANC received about 63 percent of the popular vote. According to the interim constitution, however, the ruling party would not be able to change the constitution without consultation with other parties unless it won two-thirds of the vote. Falling just short of the 66 percent needed, the ANC would now have to work with other political parties in writing the new permanent constitution.

THE END OF APARTHEID

On May 9, 1994, the South African parliament voted to select the nation's president. It surprised no one that Nelson Mandela emerged the winner. But with this vote of confidence in Mandela came a daunting responsibility. For generations, black

South Africans had campaigned for change. They were now in no mood for patience. They wanted the social and economic progress so many had fought and died for to happen immediately. Mandela also had to think about white South Africans. Somehow, he had to strip them of the unearned privileges they had known all their lives, without so alienating them that they unleashed new waves of violence. In his inauguration address,

THE SOUTH AFRICAN NATIONAL ANTHEM

Section 4 of the 1996 constitution of South Africa declared that the country would have a new and, in many ways, unique national anthem. The new anthem combined two songs already well known in South Africa. One was "Die Stem van Suid-Afrika," meaning "The Call of South Africa" in Afrikaans. It had been the official anthem during most of the apartheid era. The other was "Nkosi Sikelel' iAfrika" ("God Bless Africa"), which was written by Enoch Sontonga, a Methodist schoolteacher, in 1897. Originally sung as a hymn during church services, it became the anthem of the African National Congress.

The new anthem also paid tribute to South Africa's multicultural and multilingual society. It included lyrics in five different languages. The first two stanzas are in three African languages (Xhosa, Zulu, and Sesotho), the third stanza in Afrikaans, and the final one in English.

(Complete English translation)

Nkosi sikelel' Afrika	Lord bless Africa
Maluphakanyisw' uphondo lwayo	May her glory be lifted high

Mandela struck a positive note, declaring how all citizens, whatever their race, should be inspired by the courage of those who had made the new South Africa possible: "We dedicate this day to all the heroes and heroines in this country and the rest of the world who sacrificed in many ways and surrendered their lives so that we could be free. Their dreams have become reality. Freedom is their reward."[3]

Yizwa imithandazo yethu	Hear our petitions
Nkosi sikelela, thina lusapho lwayo.	Lord bless us, your children
Morena boloka setjhaba sa heso,	Lord we ask You to protect our nation
O fedise dintwa le matshwenyeho,	Intervene and end all conflicts
O se boloke, O se boloke setjhaba sa heso,	Protect us, protect our nation
Setjhaba sa South Afrika—South Afrika.	Protect South Africa, South Africa
Uit die blou van onse hemel,	Out of the blue of our heavens
Uit die diepte van ons see,	Out of the depths of our seas
Oor ons ewige gebergtes,	Over our everlasting mountains
Waar die kranse antwoord gee,	Where the echoing crags resound
Sounds the call to come together,	Sounds the call to come together,
And united we shall stand,	And united we shall stand,
Let us live and strive for freedom,	Let us live and strive for freedom,
In South Africa our land.	In South Africa our land.*

*"National Anthem." Department of Foreign Affairs, The Republic of South Africa. http://www.dfa.gov.za/department/National/anthem.html?include=symbols/anthem.html.

The newly installed parliament then set about drafting the new South African constitution. Completed in 1996, it was one of the most progressive constitutions in the world. Written in simple, easily understood language, it outlined ideas of democracy, equality, and freedom similar to those found in the Constitution of the United States. But its list of fundamental rights also included the right to higher education, to decent housing, and to strike for improved working conditions. It also called for equal rights for women and homosexuals and established an obligation to protect the environment and all children from abuse and neglect.

The adoption of the South African constitution marked a historic moment. Apartheid—the horrific moral blight that had so long tainted the nation—was finally dead and buried. In its place was a framework for a government that would treat all its citizens as equals. Even more amazing, this massive change had occurred without an all-out civil war. After centuries of violence and bitterness, the peaceful transfer of power from South Africa's white minority to its black majority seemed like nothing short of a miracle.

Apartheid's Legacy

In his inauguration speech, President Nelson Mandela hailed the new South Africa as a "rainbow nation"[1]—words that echoed the 39-year-old Freedom Charter, which declared that "South Africa belongs to all who live in it, black and white."[2] To most South Africans, the end of apartheid promised the beginning of a brighter future for their nation. Yet, at the same time, many people also feared that the ghosts of the past threatened any effort to move forward.

THE TRUTH AND RECONCILIATION COMMISSION

With this fear in mind, the parliament passed the Promotion of National Unity and Reconciliation Act in 1995. The law—intended to help all South Africans come to terms with the apartheid era—called for a commission to investigate politically motivated human rights violations that had occurred between 1960 and 1994.

Mandela selected 17 representatives to serve on what became known as the Truth and Reconciliation Commission (TRC). The comission was led by Desmond Tutu, the internationally famed clergyman and anti-apartheid activist who had been awarded the Nobel Peace Prize in 1984.

For more than two and a half years, the commissioners sifted through 22,000 written statements from victims and witnesses of political crimes. They told horrendous stories of South Africans—mostly black—who were raped, tortured, beaten, mutilated, and murdered. Thousands of statements also recounted how families were torn from their homes and prisoners were detained without charges. About 10 percent of the victims' complaints were discussed in hearings that were broadcast across South Africa on television and radio. A few testimonies dealt with high profile cases, such as the murder of Stephen Biko. Most, however, were offered by ordinary South Africans, who with great emotion described how their bodies had been battered and their lives nearly destroyed by the cruelties unleashed by apartheid.

GRANTING AMNESTY

The TRC also considered more than 7,000 requests for amnesty submitted by police officers, soldiers, and other citizens who committed acts of violence to further the goals of the apartheid regime. The TRC was authorized to forgive these crimes if the commission concluded that the offenses were politically, rather than personally, motivated and that the petitioners had told the truth.

In the end, the TRC granted amnesty to only about 850 applicants. Tutu stated that letting their acts go unpunished in exchange for their honest testimonies constituted "another kind of justice—a restorative justice which is concerned not so much with punishment as with correcting imbalances, restor-

On March 21, 2003, Archbishop Desmond Tutu *(left)* hands over the final report of the Truth and Reconciliation Commission to South African President Thabo Mbeki.

ing broken relationships—with healing, harmony and reconciliation."[3] Still, some South Africans were angered that these killers, torturers, and rapists were permitted to go free. Others complained that major political leaders, such as P.W. Botha and F.W. de Klerk, were not held accountable for apartheid's murderous policies. The TRC also was criticized for its role in establishing reparations, or payments to compensate victims for their financial losses and suffering. Most reparations were very small, and many went unpaid.

Many people, however, lauded the work of the TRC. The testimonies compiled by the commission constituted the most exhaustive investigation ever made into the political crimes of any era. Even if the TRC's efforts did not achieve complete reconciliation, the investigation did help heal some of the wounds of past atrocities. In part because of the work of the TRC, the number of political crimes in South Africa dropped dramatically.

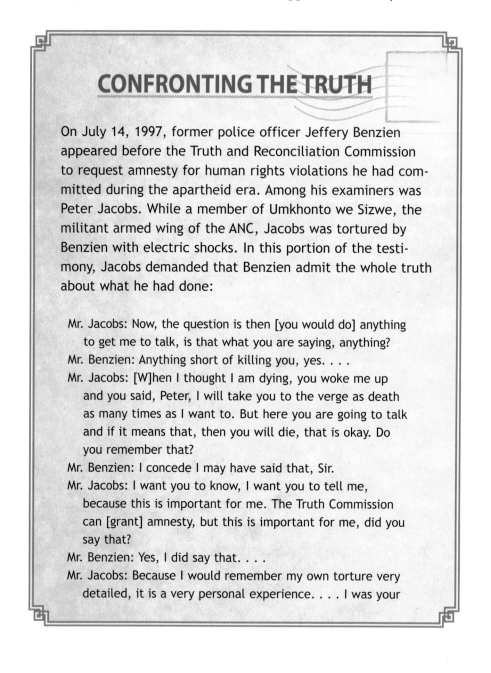

CONFRONTING THE TRUTH

On July 14, 1997, former police officer Jeffery Benzien appeared before the Truth and Reconciliation Commission to request amnesty for human rights violations he had committed during the apartheid era. Among his examiners was Peter Jacobs. While a member of Umkhonto we Sizwe, the militant armed wing of the ANC, Jacobs was tortured by Benzien with electric shocks. In this portion of the testimony, Jacobs demanded that Benzien admit the whole truth about what he had done:

Mr. Jacobs: Now, the question is then [you would do] anything to get me to talk, is that what you are saying, anything?

Mr. Benzien: Anything short of killing you, yes. . . .

Mr. Jacobs: [W]hen I thought I am dying, you woke me up and you said, Peter, I will take you to the verge as death as many times as I want to. But here you are going to talk and if it means that, then you will die, that is okay. Do you remember that?

Mr. Benzien: I concede I may have said that, Sir.

Mr. Jacobs: I want you to know, I want you to tell me, because this is important for me. The Truth Commission can [grant] amnesty, but this is important for me, did you say that?

Mr. Benzien: Yes, I did say that. . . .

Mr. Jacobs: Because I would remember my own torture very detailed, it is a very personal experience. . . . I was your

REPAIRING A NATION

While South Africans were dealing with the emotional repercussions of apartheid, they also were working to rebuild their
nation. Apartheid had wreaked havoc with the country's

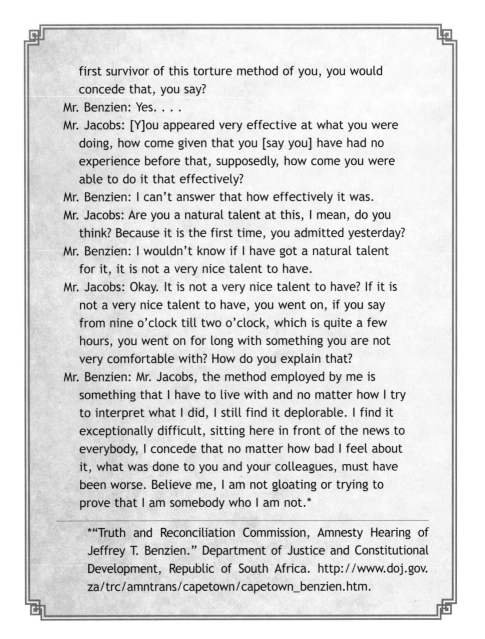

first survivor of this torture method of you, you would
concede that, you say?

Mr. Benzien: Yes. . . .

Mr. Jacobs: [Y]ou appeared very effective at what you were
doing, how come given that you [say you] have had no
experience before that, supposedly, how come you were
able to do it that effectively?

Mr. Benzien: I can't answer that how effectively it was.

Mr. Jacobs: Are you a natural talent at this, I mean, do you
think? Because it is the first time, you admitted yesterday?

Mr. Benzien: I wouldn't know if I have got a natural talent
for it, it is not a very nice talent to have.

Mr. Jacobs: Okay. It is not a very nice talent to have? If it is
not a very nice talent to have, you went on, if you say
from nine o'clock till two o'clock, which is quite a few
hours, you went on for long with something you are not
very comfortable with? How do you explain that?

Mr. Benzien: Mr. Jacobs, the method employed by me is
something that I have to live with and no matter how I try
to interpret what I did, I still find it deplorable. I find it
exceptionally difficult, sitting here in front of the news to
everybody, I concede that no matter how bad I feel about
it, what was done to you and your colleagues, must have
been worse. Believe me, I am not gloating or trying to
prove that I am somebody who I am not.*

*"Truth and Reconciliation Commission, Amnesty Hearing of
Jeffrey T. Benzien." Department of Justice and Constitutional
Development, Republic of South Africa. http://www.doj.gov.
za/trc/amntrans/capetown/capetown_benzien.htm.

political, social, and economic health. Mandela's government therefore faced a wealth of challenges in trying to craft a modern and stable post-apartheid South Africa.

The 1996 constitution itself ended many past abuses. The government was forbidden from censoring the press, torturing prisoners, detaining citizens without pressing criminal charges, and seizing houses and other property without cause. The constitution also lifted all restrictions on people's freedom of movement inside or outside the country. South Africans of any race could now live wherever they wanted.

The Mandela government also initiated the ambitious Reconstruction and Development Program (RDP). By funding local development projects, the RDP sought to improve health care, housing, and education for all South Africans. Especially in rural areas, it increased access to health clinics and to clean drinking water. In the townships, the program helped bring electricity to numerous homes and offices. The government also subsidized the construction of more than one million low-cost houses, which were nicknamed "Mandela homes." These modest four-room houses were a vast improvement over the shacks and shanties many black South Africans had previously called home.

The South African parliament also turned its attention to land reform. In its first piece of legislation after the 1994 election, it invited black citizens who had been stripped of their property under apartheid to make formal land claims. The law sought to reverse the effects of the Natives Land Act of 1913, which had given whites control over most of the land in South Africa. In practice, however, the redistribution of land proved to be a very slow and difficult process. Many claimants became frustrated when the new government seemed unable to restore their land rights as promised.

Undoing the damage done by apartheid was challenging in many other areas as well. Under apartheid, the government had neglected to build needed roads and bridges, especially in regions with large black populations. The Mandela government tried to build up the national infrastructure, but it struggled to find the funds needed to make these improvements. Apartheid policies also had created massive environmental problems, because mining and industrial companies had been allowed to pollute areas designated for blacks. As a result, the post-apartheid government was faced with the difficult and costly cleanup of these environmentally devastated areas.

A NEW ECONOMIC PLAN

Perhaps the most difficult challenge for post-apartheid South Africa was promoting economic growth. Apartheid policies had created a largely untrained and uneducated workforce. In addition, the entire economy had been based on keeping workers' wages low. The new government wanted to raise wages to help the poor. Doing so, however, was sure to scare away foreign investors. Without foreign investment, the South African economy would fall apart.

With that in mind, the Mandela government abandoned the RDP in favor of a new economic program—Growth, Employment, and Redistribution (GEAR) in 1996. The GEAR strategy tried to attract foreign businesses and investments to South Africa by limiting regulations and restrictions on their dealings. By improving the South African economy overall, the ultimate goal of GEAR was to create more jobs at higher wages. At the same time, it attempted to rein in government spending on economic development programs intended to help poor and struggling South Africans.

GEAR was strongly supported by Thabo Mbeki, who became president after Nelson Mandela retired from politics in 1999. Mbeki believed that GEAR could create an "African Renaissance." He envisioned all of Africa pulling itself out of poverty, with South Africa leading the way. But many South

Africans believed the program was too pro-business and complained that it did little for the common worker. The growing disillusionment with the direction of the nation caused a split in the ANC, which remained South Africa's most powerful political party. This rift became more pronounced after Mandela left office. Mandela was such a revered national hero that people were hesitant to criticize him. But after Mbeki took over, they felt freer to voice their complaints about the new post-apartheid government.

THE AIDS CRISIS

Mbeki gave his critics plenty of ammunition with his handling of a severe health crisis. By the late 1990s, South Africa was suffering from an epidemic of the acquired immune deficiency syndrome (AIDS). In 1998, the life expectancy of South Africans had been 60. Experts projected that because of the rapid spread of AIDS, that number would drop to 40 by the year 2010. The huge number of deaths from AIDS left many women as single parents and children as orphans. Their tragic situations placed an extra burden on social services, which the government was already struggling to fund.

As the AIDS crisis grew, Mbeki made a series of bizarre public statements about the disease and the epidemic. He maintained that the problem of AIDS in South Africa had been overblown. Ignoring all medical evidence, Mbeki also questioned whether the human immunodeficiency virus (HIV) caused AIDS and suggested that the retroviral drugs used to combat HIV were possibly toxic. His health minister promoted a medicine made from garlic and beetroot instead. Health experts around the world were appalled by Mbeki's strange response to an epidemic that was killing 350,000 of his citizens a year. Within South Africa, his statements spawned a social movement called the Treatment Action Campaign. Activists involved in the movement successfully sued the government to force public hospitals to provide free retroviral drugs to HIV patients.

GIVING UP ON THE GOVERNMENT

South Africans were also highly critical of the government's inability to address another crisis—the country's staggering rate of violent crime. High unemployment and horrible poverty led to an epidemic of robberies, burglaries, and carjackings. Although most of these crimes were financially motivated, the rage unleashed by the injustices of apartheid often led criminals to inflict appalling violence on their victims. In one high-profile case, Marike de Klerk, the former wife of F.W. de Klerk, was stabbed and strangled to death in her home in 2001.

The huge number of guns in South Africa also contributed to the crime wave. During the apartheid era, whites armed themselves out of fear of a black rebellion. In addition, many weapons were smuggled into the country from ANC bases in Angola and Mozambique. The police, used to focusing their energy on battling political activists, were not prepared to deal effectively with criminals and gangs. Many gang members were young men who had been engaged in the armed struggle against apartheid. Unable to find jobs in the new South Africa, they turned to gangs as a source of prestige and power.

The Mbeki government also drew criticism for its mismanagement of necessary services. Symbolic of its failings was a disastrous malfunction at the Koeberg Nuclear Power Station on February 19, 2006. For weeks, the power plant was shut down, leaving much of the country without a source of electricity. Businesses closed down, gas pumps and traffic lights stopped working, and looters ran wild. Many angry citizens complained that the government was so incompetent it could not even keep lights on in the major city of Cape Town.

In the summer of 2008, outrage over the high unemployment rate during Mbeki's presidency led to a horrifying series of riots. In several cities, mobs took out their anger on poor immigrants. Before the riots were quelled, 56 immigrants were dead, and thousands had fled the country. The violence threatened the nation's tourism industry, which led to still more economic woes.

MBEKI VERSUS ZUMA

By that time, many black South Africans had given up on Mbeki. They instead placed their faith in Jacob Zuma, who had served as Mbeki's deputy president. The two men had once been friends. But when Zuma, a shrewd politician and rousing speaker, began to draw more support from frustrated workers and the poor, he and Mbeki became political rivals. In 2005, Mbeki fired Zuma after one of Zuma's advisers was convicted of bribery. Zuma himself was accused of rape. In a controversial trial, Zuma was eventually found not guilty.

Strangely, these scandals only seemed to increase Zuma's popularity. Those tired of Mbeki's rule saw Zuma as their savior—the best and maybe last hope for creating a new South Africa that would address their concerns and serve their needs. Mbeki was disturbed by Zuma's rise, especially because his own presidency was coming to an end. His second term would be over in 2009, and by the terms of the constitution, he was not allowed to run for a third. In a bid to retain at least some power, Mbeki campaigned to become the leader of the ANC in 2007. To his chagrin, Zuma won the position instead.

Mbeki's government responded by making formal charges against Zuma, who was indicted on racketeering, corruption, money laundering, and fraud, in connection with bribes he had allegedly taken from a French company that was selling arms to South Africa. Not surprisingly, Zuma's supporters claimed the prosecution was motivated purely by politics. They angrily accused Mbeki of trumping up charges just to destroy his long-time rival. The controversy left the ANC party in tatters. Its membership was torn in two between those supporting Mbeki and those supporting Zuma.

THE END OF MBEKI'S REGIME

On September 12, 2008, Judge Chris Nicholson set aside the case against Zuma. He made no decisions about Zuma's guilt or innocence. He instead claimed that the prosecution had grossly mishandled the case. Striking an angry tone, the judge maintained that the charges against Zuma were politically motivated, although he also demanded that they be addressed in a formal inquiry. Nicholson dramatically declared, "Only a commission of inquiry can properly rid our land of this cancer that is devouring the body politic and the reputation for integrity built so assiduously after the fall of apartheid."[4] Zuma and his supporters took the judge's words as complete vindication. A crowd decked out in Zuma T-shirts cheered as their leader emerged from the courthouse. After singing a Zulu war song, Zuma shouted out, "It is a victory for the judiciary; it is a victory for our democracy; it is a victory for our justice system."[5]

No one knew for sure what would happen next. Supporters of Mbeki vowed to revive the case against Zuma, while supporters of Zuma promised to fight to the death if Zuma were imprisoned. Many feared the government would fall apart if the battle between Mbeki and Zuma continued any longer. They worried that Zuma would be elected president in 2009 but a revived criminal trial would prevent him from taking office. If that happened, the whole country might erupt in civil war.

To prevent that disaster, the executive committee of the ANC put heavy pressure on Mbeki to resign from the presidency. Just over a week after Nicholson's declaration, Mbeki appeared on national television. In a 14-minute speech, Mbeki announced that he would step down. Zuma's ally Kgalema Motlanthe was selected to serve out Mbeki's second term in

Two schoolgirls attend tennis practice in 1992 at Brebner High School in Bloemfontein, one of the first schools to push integration. Although legal racial equality has been established in South Africa, many challenges remain for Mandela's fledgling "rainbow nation."

preparation for the next year's election, in which Zuma was sure to emerge the victor.

DESPAIR AND HOPE

As expected, the ANC won the next election, and on May 9, 2009, Jacob Zuma was sworn in as the fourth president of South Africa since apartheid was dismantled. After apartheid, many South Africans—both black and white—had had high hopes for their country, the great "rainbow nation" Mandela had promised. Now many were overwhelmed with feelings of despair as their country was engulfed by political uncertainty, raging crime, epidemic disease, and economic upheaval.

Others, however, were less alarmed. They claimed that the process of creating the new South Africa was not over. In fact, it was just beginning. Apartheid had left the country in shambles. It was hardly surprising that molding South Africa into a modern and prosperous democracy did not happen in an instant. It was a project that would require time, energy, and patience for many years to come.

In this sense, the Mbeki-Zuma drama was itself a cause of hope. That such a heated political battle could be resolved peacefully demonstrated that the nation had already taken great strides away from its tragic past and toward a better future. As Adam Habib, deputy vice chancellor of the University of Johannesburg, told the *New York Times* in 2008, "Our democracy is only 14 years old. Rather than calling this a crisis, people ought to ask how our institutions came together so well in so short a time."[6]

CHRONOLOGY

1652	The Dutch East India Company founds a settlement at present-day Cape Town.
1806	Great Britain takes control over the Cape region.
1838	Dutch farmers abandon the eastern Cape in the Great Trek.
1886	Gold is discovered near what is now Johannesburg.
1899-1902	The British fight and defeat the Boers in the South African War.

TIMELINE

1976
Hundreds of student protesters are killed during the Soweto massacre.

1948
National Party wins control of the South African parliament.

1948 **1976**

1950s
South African government enacts a series of apartheid laws.

1964
Eight African National Congress (ANC) leaders, including Nelson Mandela, are sentenced to life in prison following the Rivonia trial.

1955
The Congress of the People approves the Freedom Charter.

1912   The South African Native National Congress, later renamed the African National Congress (ANC), is established.

1914   The National Party (NP) is founded.

1948   The NP wins control of the South African parliament.

1950s   The South African government enacts a series of apartheid laws.

1955   The Congress of the People approves the Freedom Charter.

1960   Police kill dozens of demonstrators in the township of Sharpeville.

1978
Prime Minister P.W. Botha enacts the Total Strategy against political opponents.

2008
South Africans riot to protest the influx of immigrant laborers; President Thabo Mbeki resigns following a power struggle with Jacob Zuma.

1978

2008

1985
The South African government declares an official state of emergency.

1994
The ANC wins South Africa's first democratic election; Mandela is named the new president.

1996–1998
Truth and Reconciliation Commission hearings are held.

1964	Eight ANC leaders, including Nelson Mandela, are sentenced to life in prison following the Rivonia trial.
1976	Hundreds of student protesters are killed during the Soweto massacre.
1977	South African Students' Organization leader Stephen Biko is murdered in police custody.
1978	Prime Minister P.W. Botha enacts the Total Strategy against all political opponents.
1985	The South African government declares an official state of emergency.
1989	F.W. de Klerk becomes South Africa's president.
1990	Nelson Mandela and other political prisoners are released from jail.
1993	Mandela and de Klerk are awarded the Nobel Peace Prize.
1994	The ANC wins South Africa's first democratic election; Mandela is named the new South African president.
1996-1998	Truth and Reconciliation Commission hearings are held.
1999	Mandela retires from politics; Thabo Mbeki becomes South Africa's president.
2003	South Africa becomes the country with the largest number of HIV-infected citizens.
2008	South Africans riot to protest the influx of immigrant laborers; President Mbeki resigns following a power struggle with Jacob Zuma.

NOTES

CHAPTER 1

1. Anthony Sampson, *Mandela: The Authorized Biography*. New York: Alfred A. Knopf, 1999, p. 397.
2. Ibid.
3. Nelson Mandela, *Long Walk to Freedom: The Autobiography of Nelson Mandela*. Boston: Little, Brown & Company, 1994, p. 490.
4. Ibid.
5. Ibid.
6. Ibid., p. 491.
7. Ibid.
8. Ibid.
9. Ibid., p. 492.
10. Ibid.
11. Ibid., p. 493.
12. Nancy L. Clark and William H. Worger, *South Africa: The Rise and Fall of Apartheid*. Harlow, England: Pearson Education, Ltd., 2004, p. 151.
13. Ibid.
14. Ibid.
15. Ibid., p. 152.
16. Ibid.
17. Ibid.

CHAPTER 2

1. Nigel Worden, *The Making of Modern South Africa: Conquest, Apartheid, Democracy*, 4th ed. Malden, Mass.: Blackwell Publishing, 2007, p. 13.

2. Lindsay Michie Eades, *The End of Apartheid in South Africa*. Westport, Conn.: Greenwood Press, 1999, p. 5.

CHAPTER 3

1. Clark and Worger, *South Africa*, p. 22.
2. Ibid., p. 24.

CHAPTER 4

1. Ibid., p. 41.
2. Ibid., p. 42.
3. Ibid., p. 43.
4. Ibid., p. 52.
5. Worden, *The Making of Modern South Africa*, p. 106.
6. Clark and Worger, *South Africa*, p. 52.
7. "Protest and Resistance Through the Rivonia Trial (1964)." South Africa: Overcoming Apartheid, Building Democracy, http://overcomingapartheid.msu.edu/unit.php?id=17&page=2.

CHAPTER 5

1. Clark and Worger, *South Africa*, p. 60.
2. Ibid., p. 65.
3. Ibid., p. 74.

CHAPTER 6

1. Eades, *The End of Apartheid in South Africa*, p. 22.

2. Clark and Worger, *South Africa*, p. 92.

3. Ibid.

CHAPTER 7

1. Ibid., p. 105.
2. Ibid., p. 106.
3. Ibid., p. 110.

CHAPTER 8

1. Ibid., p. 154.
2. Ibid., p. 134.
3. "Exploring the Truth and Reconciliation Commission." South Africa: Overcoming Apartheid, Building Democracy, http://overcomingapartheid.msu.edu/unit.php?id=15.

4. Barry Bearak, "Judge Dismisses Corruption Charges Against Leader of South Africa's Ruling Party," *New York Times*, September 12, 2008, http://www.nytimes.com/2008/09/13/world/africa/13zuma.html.

5. Ibid.

6. Barry Bearak, "Post-Apartheid South Africa Enters Anxious Era," *New York Times*, October 5, 2008, http://www.nytimes.com/2008/10/06/world/africa/06safrica.html.

BIBLIOGRAPHY

BOOKS

Clark, Nancy L., and William H. Worger. *South Africa: The Rise and Fall of Apartheid*. Harlow, England: Pearson Education Ltd., 2004.

Eades, Lindsay Michie. *The End of Apartheid in South Africa*. Westport, Conn.: Greenwood Press, 1999.

Edgar, Robert R., ed. *An African American in South Africa: The Travel Notes of Ralph J. Bunche, 28 September 1937– 1 January 1938*. Athens, Ohio: Ohio University Press, 1992.

Mandela, Nelson. *Long Walk to Freedom: The Autobiography of Nelson Mandela*. Boston: Little, Brown & Company, 1994.

The Nelson Mandela Foundation. *A Prisoner in the Garden*. New York: Viking Studio, 2006.

Sampson, Anthony. *Mandela: The Authorized Biography*. New York: Alfred A. Knopf, 1999.

Thompson, Leonard. *A History of South Africa*. 3rd ed. New Haven, Conn.: Yale University Press, 2000.

Worden, Nigel. *The Making of South Africa: Conquest, Apartheid, Democracy*. 4th ed. Malden, Mass.: Blackwell Publishing, 2007.

FURTHER RESOURCES

BOOKS

Crompton, Samuel Willard. *Desmond Tutu*. New York: Chelsea House, 2006.

Downing, David. *Apartheid in South Africa*. Chicago: Heinemann Library, 2004.

Fish, Bruce, and Becky Durost Fish. *South Africa: 1880 to the Present*. Philadelphia: Chelsea House, 2000.

Gaines, Ann Graham. *Nelson Mandela and Apartheid in World History*. Berkeley Heights, N.J.: Enslow Publishers, 2001.

Mathabane, Mark. *Kaffir Boy: The True Story of a Black Youth's Coming of Age in Apartheid South Africa*. New York: Simon & Schuster, 1986.

WEB SITES

African National Congress
  http://www.anc.org.za

Nelson Mandela Foundation
  http://www.nelsonmandela.org

Nelson Mandela National Museum
  http://www.nelsonmandelamuseum.org.za/index2.htm

South Africa: Overcoming Apartheid, Building Democracy
  http://overcomingapartheid.msu.edu/index.php

South African History Online
  http://www.sahistory.org.za/pages/index/menu.htm

Truth and Reconciliation Committee
  http://www.doj.gov.za/trc/

PICTURE CREDITS

INDEX

ABOUT THE AUTHOR

LIZ SONNEBORN is a writer living in Brooklyn, New York. A graduate of Swarthmore College, she has written more than 70 books for children and adults. Her works include *The American West*, *The Gold Rush*, *Yemen*, *A to Z of American Indian Women*, and *The Ancient Kushites*, which the African Studies Association's Children's Africana Book Awards named an Honor Book for Older Readers in 2006.